MYSTICAL REHAB and Other Occasions

Poems by Richard Harteis

ISBN: 978-1-7335400-3-2

POETS-CHOICE.COM

Poets' Choice
337 Kitemaug Road
Uncasville, Ct. 06382

Marathonfilm@gmail.com

All Rights Reserved

Library of Congress Cataloging-in-Publication Data pending

Consultant work: Barbara Shaw

Copyright © 2019, Poets Choice Publishing

MYSTICAL REHAB, and Other Occasions

Poems by Richard Harteis

"I think we are well advised to keep on nodding terms with the people we used to be, whether we find them attractive company or not. Otherwise, they turn up unannounced and surprise us, come hammering on the mind's door at 4 a.m. of a bad night and demand to know who deserted them, who betrayed them, who is going to make amends."

Joan Didion – *On Keeping a Notebook*

Dedication

These poems celebrate the life I've shared with
William, Nancy and lately, Mike
with great gratitude.

TABLE OF CONTENTS

p. 1 INTRODUCTION
p. 3 Intensive Care
p. 5 Reveille: 8/18/19
p. 7 Into the Wormhole
p. 9 Fake Eggs Go Flying All Over
p. 10 TMI *
p. 11 Lights Out
p. 12 Serengeti Blues
p. 13 Vespers
p. 14 Discharge
p. 15 NEW CENTURY POEMS
P. 16 The Announcement of the Human Genome Project's Completion
P. 17 Aubade for Alva
p. 18 Aubade Part II
p. 19 Hyposmia
p. 20 Lullaby
p. 21 Suicide Note
p. 22 Florida Farewell
p. 24 Now Comes Dream
p. 25 If You Returned
p. 26 After the World Changed
p. 27 At the Aquarium
p. 28 Armageddon
p. 29 Desert Song
p. 30 Second Chance Moon
p. 31 Autumn Postcard
p. 32 If I Were William Meredith
p. 33 In My Tomb Tonight
p. 34 In Passing
p. 35 A Little Summer Music
p. 37 He Goes to Proust and Einstein Looking at Time
p. 39 Objet Trouve: in the Faust Lane
p. 41 911- A Year Later
p. 42 Totem
P 43 Good Friday
p. 44 Postcard
p. 45 September 11, 2004
p. 47 Uxorial
p. 48 Treat Time
p. 49 Notes on a Hearty Merlot
p. 50 Homage to Ezra Pound
p. 51 At The Opera
p. 52 Farewell Superman

p. 53 Housekeeping
p. 56 Cat Burglary

p. 58 Death of Pope
p. 60 Portraits
p. 62 High Style at J.C. Pennay's
p. 64 The Lone Swan
p. 65 Thank You Note to John Rigo
p. 66 Preparing for Death
p. 67 The Speech Therapist Makes a House Call
p. 68 In Vino Veritas
p. 69 Colony Collapse Disorder
p. 70 A Gradate of York Catholic High School
p. 74 Memorial Day, 2007
p. 79 Legacy
p. 80 Homework
p. 81 Adrift
p. 83 Anecdotal
p. 84 Pathetic Fallacy
p. 85 After the Rain
p. 86 The Deer are After the Apples Again
p. 87 Counsel
p. 88 Apology
p. 89 Vin Triste
p. 91 Gardening
p. 92 Aubade
p. 93 Quandry
p. 94 Moot Epiphany
p. 95 After Berry Picking
p. 96 Procrastination
p. 97 Night Flower
p. 98 Another February 14th
p. 99 IDLING AT RIVERRUN
P. 100 Board Meeting
p. 101 Café Bistro, Johan Strauss Vienna
p. 102 William's Notion of Courage, 1945
p. 103 Pirate's Ball
p. 104 Bulgarian Translation
p. 106 Plein Air
p. 109 Coffee Poem
p. 109 Twenty One Polo Horses Dead from Mysterious Illness
p. THE REVENANT
P. 111 The Revenant
p. 112 Anniversary, for William
p. 113 Skunk Hour
p.114 Night Light for Daisy
p. 115 Sensory Perception
p. 116 Daisy Auf Naxos
p. 117 True Adventure
p. 118 At the Vet
p. 119 Daisy Chain

P. 120 Bedtime
p. 121 July 4th
p. 123 Camouflage
p. 124 Daisy Reads Bambi the Riot Act
p. 125 Summer of Rainbows
p. 126 Getting Attuned by My Reike Master
p. 127 All She Has
p. 128 Busted at Misquamicut State Park
p. 130 Cocktails
p. 131 Day Trader
p. 133 Juan
p. 134 Dancing Lesson
p. 135 Multiple Choice Lyric
p. 136 For Betsy
p. 137 Suite Insomnia
p. 138 Ms. Daisy's Retort
p. 139 Letter from Tucker on Cowboy's death
p. 140 "Honey, when is mosquitos over?"
p. 142 Leftovers
p. 144 Little Needle from the Peanut Gallery
p. 145 Undercounted Unemployed
p. 146 Little Panegyric for Gracie,
p. 147 Q and A
p. 149 Winter Verse for his Brother
p. 150 Eventide
p. 152 Sex Education
p. 153 Autumn on the River
p. 155 The Cricket Sings the Blues
p. 156 Grace
p. 157 Wind Over Water
p. 158 Post Coitus at the Texas Roadhouse
p. 160 The Mind
p. 161 Meanwhile, Condo President goes Dada (rhymes with gaga)
p. 163 Writer's Prayer
p. 164 Lullaby for David
p. 165 Dream Lover
p. 166 To His Muse
p. 167 Assisted Living
p. 169 The Poet William Meredith
p. 171 Hirsutism
p. 173 CGD*
p. 175 Miniature
p. 177 Turning 65
p. 178 Cosmic Circle
p. 180 Podiatry
P. 181 911 119
p. 182 Margot Parrot from Catherine Hull's Obituary

p. 183 Busy
p. 184 Animal Trainer
p. 185 Daisy wakes from her Nightmare
p. 186 Boot Camp – Cassis
p. 189 Taking the Auspices
p. 191 Poetry
p. 193 Ava Maria Redux

p. 195 Poor Reception
p. 197 Ars Poetica
p. 198 That's What I Like about You
p. 199 The Onion Knows The Chef is Thinking Salad
p. 200 Gay Blues
p. 201 Time collapses contemplating the
 anniversary of William Meredith's death today
p. 203 Notes to the Dog Sitter
p. 204 Gaffe
p. 205 Second Shift
p. 206 Euthanasia
p. 208 Living Will
p. 209 The Morning After
p. 210 Daniel, I'm Sorry When I Visited Your School
p. 211 In the High Country
p. 212 At the Sink
p. 213 FYEO
p. 214 Call your Mother
p. 215 Les deux à la fois
p. 216 208 Both
p. 217 The Hive
p. 219 Post Card: Sozopol at Sunset
p. 220 Arrival, or the Beginning of the End
p. 223 The Sunflowers
p. 224 10.7.2013 in preparation for Krassi's 75 birthday
p. 225 Summer Animals
p. 226 Advent
p. 227 Patrick's Missed the Forsythia
p. 228 Friday before Easter
p. 230 Nike
p. 231 4:30 A.M.
p. 232 For Graeme Beryn's Old Computer
p. 233 After Dinner
p. 234 Winter Valentine
p. 235 The Peacock at Bachkovo Monastery
p. 236 Blow Jack, Blow

- p. 237 Burgeoning
- p. 238 Compassion
- p. 239 Fall Moon
- p. 240 The First Firefly of Summer
- p. 241 Kudos for Gracie
- p. 242 For Gracie, New Angel in Annapolis
- p. 243 Holiday Supper
- p. 244 Labor Day
- p. 246 Night Walk
- p. 247 Opioid Song
- p. 248 Note to Roger
- p. 249 Triptych
- p. 251 Stopping by a Virgin Park At Dusk
- p. 252 For Lyubomir Levchev
- P. 253 Lullaby
- p. 254 Old Business, Newt Business
- p. 255 A Couple of Lifted Malaproprisms
- p. 256 Sunday Mass
- p. 258 The Indian Magi Remembers: Caspar
- p. 259 Walking the Dog
- p. 261 Sandyhook Revisited
- p. 263 About the Cover

Introduction

Years ago, when I asked my friend, the newly anointed Poet Laureate of Maryland, Grace Cavalieri if she minded that critics paid little attention to her work, she said to me, "I just keep writin' 'em." So it is with most writers I guess, the writing has to be its own reward. Students often day dream of being discovered like Emily Dickinson long after their death and loaded into the canon of American literature. Until then, they protest that they are just writing for themselves.

When I published a new and collected group of poems titled PROVENCE with blurbs from many of the archangels of the poetry world – Wilbur, Merrill, Swenson, Jacobsen, Ed Hirsch, etc., Michael Collier offered an assessment, "you must be very glad to have all these poems in print." It sounded like damning with faint praise at the time, but the comment makes sense as I put together years and years of unpublished poems just written when the itch arose, before even the sun, and insomnia kept me turning an idea or line over and over in my head precluding sleep. When it was over, like a little orgasm, and the muse and I were free to retire, there seemed to be no need to do much more with it than tip it into an email for friends like Gracie, or Scott, or Nancy. Lately, such encounters with the muse were a kind of therapy, as I lay claustrophobic for a month in the Mystic Health and RehabilitationCenter.

I was flying back triumphant from Las Vegas where my screen play had won at an important film festival when two days later, I discovered I couldn't walk. Thinking I had broken my hip, I asked my noble roommate, Mike to get me to the hospital. Turns out I had forgotten about the rule against stopping blood thinners when making a long flight, and my legs had filled up with clots top to bottom. Both of them.

Eight hours later, four surgeons apparently saved my legs and my life, though 'reconciliation was their long difficult work," as William Meredith says of his and his sister's acceptance of their parents' foibles, and I ponder where the road takes me now. I'm not sure what the future will bring, but I'm glad to be limping around, insomniac yet again, wondering if I should put all these occasional poems to bed. "Here lies one whose name was writ in water," a line John Keats apparently drafted for his tombstone. Sure, I am no John Keats nor was meant to be. I'm already three times as old as he was at death, and am hardly a third of the poet he was if you can quantify these things. But

Collier's injunction makes sense to me at this point in my life. Too many sleepless nights, too many metaphors and heart breaks and longings might be recorded if only to "remind me of the man I am," as dear Stanley says in his poem, "Touch Me." And in another, "I am not done with my changes." He also says in an interview with Charlie Rose how difficult it is to write poems as you get older. The great risk is simply in repeating oneself.

In other collections, I have grouped poems into themes as was the editor's preference: love, work, play; edge of consciousness, border of memory, and so on. But those categories seem a bit contrived now. I've organized the poems in a limited way, but my goal here is a simple chronology of the poems as they came to me, a to z, starting with a number from the month-long recuperation at Mystic Healthcare and Rehabilitation Center. I hope they will be something like a stream of consciousness you can dip into possibly to find a lucky stone, or something worth keeping.

I'm fortunate to have a little press where I can air out my closet. Most writers have to curtsey and solicit the good graces of this publisher or that. But there is no shame in self publication. Who cares? "I just keep writin' ' em," as Gracie says.

AUGUST 2019 MYSTICAL REHABILITATION

Intensive Care

For Sam

When the surgical incisions
in my groin have healed, I'll let
a tattoo artist turn them into arrows
for the slings and arrows one must
face - not exactly elegant dueling
scars, but reminders of what I have
faced with some small courage, will
tie me into life like an ageing animal
mother who a surgeon has marked
with a C-section as she walks the
long road with fellow pilgrims.

This morning Jeffrey Epstein
The schmuck, lies cold and
wizened on a slab of marble,
gone the palatial pleasure
palaces, his onanistic
highlife with the
rich and famous.

"Are you Italian," I ask Sam
as he empties the commode
and lifts my legs into bed.

"I'm Jewish," he says,
with pride.

He's like the beautiful
Gerasim who inspires
epiphany for Ivan Ilyich as
he lies dying.

At the wake, mourners will offer
polite condolences before they
retire to the salon for cards and
cake and vodka - "believe me..."

But for me and Ivan Ilyich, this boy
is the window into light, simple, sacred.

Reveille:8/18/19

The nursing shifts fly in and out like
water over Niagara Falls. Who's
counting? Sandra, Darcinia, Asha.
You barely wake up and here
comes a whole new crew.
Doris will rearrange your
flowers and clean up the
urinal which has spilled on
the floor. Suddenly, there is
breakfast: fake eggs and a
croissant turned into a biscuit
hard enough for your dog to play
with. The battery in the clock on
the wall has died and the hour is
fixed at 5:05. It's always
5 o'clock somewhere they say,
but there will be no Mimosa for
me this morning. Still, you are
alive. It is your birthday and
behind the drawn curtain,
gray seems to be blossoming
into blue. If there is
enough blue to make a pair of
pants, my mother always said, it
is going to be a good day. How
much blue is blue, I wonder.

Where did she get her meteorological skills and seamstress talent? So much magic in the world.

Into the Wormhole

For Jack Harte

In Ireland once, on a
westernmost island I met a
family who treated their baby
girl like a princess among
their other royal children,
despite her palsy. And

In a pub, the most beautiful
boy I have ever met was
drinking Guinness late into the
night as they announced the
winners of the fishing
competition. He told me how he
had lost a testicle to cancer,
spoke of it as though It were
the most natural thing in the world.

When he said to me how
much he loved his father
and mother, he began to
cry, and an angel walked
through the room.

In Nancy's lower
bathroom, she has a
picture of grasses

growing lush and green

and underneath, the Irish

saying: "It is in the shelter

of each other that we

live."

      Now is this hospital bed

In this dark hour, I turn

over to dictate this

memory despite the

pain, grateful For the

love I have felt in this

memory, the long-

distance shelter from

this westernmost island.

Fake Eggs Go Flying

The green button makes the chair go up ,
But if you push it to the max, the table
on which your breakfast has been laid
Gets knocked all to hell. Now my socks are
filled with milk and goodness knows when a
shower is in the offing.

The head of the kitchen hears the crash
and I try to assure him that I'm not
making a statement about the "fake eggs,"
the Donald Trump special.

"These are real eggs," he says.

"Yeah, right Glenn. Like the liquid beef
I imagine you pour into some oil to make
a Philly steak and cheese."

But no point in busting his chops.
He's got a 100 people to make breakfast for,
and I'd cut corners too if I were in his apron.

TMI *

For Mikey

Zha Zha Gabor says every orgasm counts
for a 1000 calories if you're on a diet. At this point,
I wouldn't mind losing a few pounds.

Yesterday, despite doctor's orders,
I managed to move all the parts
just to show it was still possible.
Who will love me now that I am
Frankenstein's younger brother,
I wonder, except me I suppose. I don't plan
to go to kinky pornographic websites.
Vanilla Richie will just have to make do.

I watch the ASPCA commercials and
commiserate with some poor puppy who
has lost a leg, or a pony who can't
stand up in his stall for some reason.

It is what it is, as young people say today.
Maybe if I lay off the call button,
my nurse will finish up with her other patients
and wander in with a pain pill for me.
And with luck, I'll get at least a shower.

* Too Much Information, anagram used in texting.

Lights Out

For Mikey

I lie there fresh and powdered, a clean johnny,
fantasizing about the red-haired Irish nurse
and wondering what to do about it.

I ring the call bell several times and finally
hit on the right answer. Yes, it was time to change
my dressing, and yes, another pain pill, thank you.

But I remembered the photographs she showed me
of the red-haired rug rats at home and told her finally
she needed to put me to bed properly, that I could use
a kiss because yesterday was my birthday.

Ha, ha. It worked. And she didn't hesitate to give me
a lingering peck on the cheek and pulled up my bed sheet.
Earlier, she told me she would take me to her house on
Martha's Vineyard, and I promised to take her to Block Island –
just chatting. But I got that kiss. A starting point.
You take your hope where you find it in life.

Serengeti Blues

For Lori

I seem to be a "Pradaxa Failure," the blood thinner
no longer doing its job. So, I get bumped up to the
fancy new Eliquis. I wonder if I can sue.
Who pays, who knows, who cares.

What does some poor shepherd on the Serengeti Pain
do when he has multiple DVT's? I guess he just dies
and waits for the lions to finish him off.

Here, beautiful girls come and wrap you up toe to thigh
with Ace bandages, and change your dressings twice a day –
Revenge of the Mummy. I've finally had a bm to write home about,
but at this hour in the morning, I think I'd prefer the lions.
Not too sweet, but short.

Vespers

So, Jose comes in and changes my dressing.
He goes slowly, it is that hour of the night,
and he tells me about one article he read
that made it clear to him that people who
are very rich aren't often happy. He says
he was an agnostic for many years
and then he read this article which
showed him the importance of love.

I can see that he means it, that love is working
this way in his life. And so, another moment like
the cover of my surgical book which shows a
Roman or Greek soldier looking after someone
who has lost a leg, and needs some sort help
or at least compassion.

How true it is that people live by other rules,
other philosophies, even if they aren't beautifully
clear in their own thinking.Earlier this week,
some fellow came in with a crucifix on his chest
and offered me communion. We all do what we can:
this has been a small vacation from the materialism
which rules my soul. No big particular insight here,
just this nice Peruvian guy slowly working over my leg,
taking off the nasty dressings, chatting.

Discharge

St. Paul apparently lived a sensual, damn the torpedoes life
Right up until the moment when, whack, he was hit by
lightening and finally saw the light. People who have toed the line
all their lives begrudge a deathbed conversion. That biblical story of
the boy who lived a dissolute life and finally comes home and
receives an equal share of the vineyard is supposed to take care
of these inequities. Charity is supposedly the answer.
When love comes and spiritual awakening,
"who's counting," seems to be the biblical point.

All these years I've struggled with spiritual uncertainty.
And now all this pain and nearly losing my life and legs
has changed the prism. I haven't got a leg to stand on,
ha ha. Why, the eternal question. Why this pain,
why did she die, why did this happen, why the
injustice of the torturer's drill. There is no answer
to the question. But it doesn't mean that nothing matters.

A child will want to ride a dolphin, swimming in the ocean, t
here is the proverbial sunset, purple and golden hinting
at tomorrow. The taste of chocolate, the smile of a favorite pet.

I sympathize with the biblical boy. Fair or not, I seem to be
drifting into some kind of acceptance of God's love.
It is what it is. Letting go seems a viable solution.
What do any of the whores of my youth, or nasty scheming
or pettiness's or other failures matter. Life is not a horse race.
We all get to the finish line somehow. Perhaps, for some,
a careless life is a prerequisite.

NEW CENTURY POEMS

The Announcement of the Human Genome Project's Completion

For Bettie Chu

I   Larry King Interviews the Dali Lama

"So, the guy from India is the hot one, Larry?"

Larry:

Is he like the king god, I mean IS
he the king god?

The Guy from India:

You got It Larry.
He is the king god.

II

So this disciple and master speak to us on the Larry King Live Show.
And you wonder, disciple and son, father and master. Mysteries
as old as creation, renewing themselves in symbol.

III
Tonight a kind of electric jell, light, sweet
encompasses this fair planet like vision
and Thomas Merton is Singing and Joseph
Cambell. Chardin is alive in the first sign
of the Omega Point, a breeze,
a pigeon of three colors flies in the
dark clouds over Rome. Sulphur,
yellow, rotten as sunrise over Rome.

IV

Girls beckon us from the beaches of Mars:
you want to lick the sweat from the ring
at her navel, as a starting point. She takes you
out of that heat, out of that heat.

You think of Sister Ann or the mystics
near Walden who channel through
miracle - any sweet thing imaginable.

V

Fraught with certainty
like a map, we come to again
like a coolness after Armageddon,
standing in the mist
shiver, regard the dawn
put on an electric coat
like crocodile, come to an ease...

Aubade for Alva

Alva comes
pretty and smart
right to yourheart

like the dawn, and you,
standing there in the grass
your feet wet, as you stare
at an electric sunrise,

in pink man, or
big orange,smiling,
small, lovely Alva,
rose lady.

Alba in Black

No nonsense Alva
black on tan
Cancun tan or
Martha's Vineyard
She fixes you
unrelenting, true
as the Pole Star, or
the little diamonds
on her ears

But if she smiles
then oh, the moon
floods brilliant
on the dark sea -
Alva drifting by -
night becomes day.

Hyposmia *

One nice side effect
Is that when I am

sleeping with my
beloved and accidentally
pass gas, neither of us
Is the wiser. And with
diminished hearing,
sleep becomes what it's
meant to be: oblivion.

When I was a teenager
I remember watching my mum
prepare the Thanksgiving meal,
her hand full of stuffing
deep into the naked bird.
"You know how to stuff a
Turkey, don't you Richie,"
she teased me.

"Nothing like a good
Eighteen incher to start
Your day right," I told
her once, breaking the
protocol of privacy
between a mother and
son (which nevertheless
Amused her) as we
each grew old and
were less shy about
where we had come to.

When I was younger,
I described in a poem
the mystery of falling
from her body Into life,
and then, toward the end,
the mystery of sharing the
humor of that connection –
which smelled sweet.

Hyposmia: a reduced ability to
smell and to detect odors.

Lullaby

William takes
to his delicate bed
The silent hours tip toe
cross his headboard.

The beasts of the night
take him in with their
white eyes, engulf him.

Without, mist covers
the house, fog blankets
him against the moon's
bright intrusion.

All is still, all potential
William dreams a
notion of solitude,
a dear privacy within
the velvet of his sleep,
Awaiting the day.

Suicide Note

Now I am closing up the house
Now I am saying goodbye to the world.
Now I am dreaming of a life beyond this house.

Now I am playing with death
Now I am beginning to imagine
my own death, as we all do;

No more bird song, no more color.
Nor cold or heat, or any particular
comfort. I am thinking how it

will be to be silent. The cuckoo on the
mantle will sing to no one. Winter will
settle into rock, rock to ice,
icy diamond - break your mother's
back, your own. I am closing
up the hose. There is no recourse.

Do not ask me why.

Florida Farewell

Sunset floods the marsh
neon pink and purple
vulgar, electric, primeval.

We stare at a green heron
frozen among the water lilies
transfixed as you and I, transfixed.
If I could look into your eyes,
bluer than the sky's reflection
I'd see him standing there,
patient as death, immovable.

Eyes empty of love,
We take in anything
but each other
as the sun dies
its splendid death.

On the far island
an alligator gleams
bronze and copper
with the day's last light.

Moorhens and American Coots
grieve to each other across
the Pickerelweed and Cord Grass.

A Great Egret lifts a star-shaped
foot, immobile; a lone Osprey
spies us from afar, waiting to see
what will happen between us.

It will be nothing. Again.
And like the tortoise stretching
his enormous neck, the
terrible wrenching to shed
a leathery shell he has outgrown,
this year again I'll somehow manage,
sink naked and vulnerable
back into the dark waters,
waiting for the shield to harden,
growing something out of myself
that might at last sustain me
against the night's perpetual loss.

Now Comes Dream.

You will slip through the stone walls
I've built around my day
like walking through mist, like
stepping through a film of water.

No savage dogs to keep you out.
You'll have your way with me,
you'll pin me or let me pin you,
your dear head will lie in her lap
while I watch, I'll kneel before you
as you blossom. You will smile at me.
Everything I've worked to clarify
will cloud over, every resolution
melt with your velvet touch -
How I've worked for this sleep,
how my spirit cries for respite,
how deserving of a little refuge.
Yet, will I certainly wake,
exhausted, to begin another day
with the terror of my love.

Bandit, sweet bastard.
Now I lay me down.

If You Returned

If you returned
I'd wind up
holding my
heart in a bag
the way one gathers
winter ashes from a hearth,
tight at the neck, to keep
the dust from breathing
white and filthy into a room
made fresh by spring.

If you returned
August's green would rot
like rust, grape and gooseberry
shrivel into seed like sad eyes
mourning the end of summer
for the sick crows to feed upon,
lifting off to lethargic fields,
like time, with their spoils.

You would still the bright ocean
if you came back, the waves
grow silent, sea foam cake on
pools of salt from which I'd drink
as though a tempest had ravaged
the night with sweet water and
orgasmic lightening, if only you
returned beloved.

After the WorldChanged: 911

"Hello guys,
     John was in 100 world trade center yesterday morning, on the 100th floor, at the time of the disaster. We have been everywhere looking for him. He is missing. Please pray for him, and call me when you get a chance. New York is a war zone. - Love, Cuz Bets "
     Message from Betsy the day after.

"Hi, this is John. Leave a message and we'll get right back to you."

     John's answering machine 9/13/01

Still no answer John, hello. Hello,
Please get back to me. Or,
are you on the line with death,
John, does he have you on hold -
ominous red button flashing?

Are you falling forever like dream
in a river of destruction, have you
taken your partner's hand and leapt
As the flames licked at your heels
and smoke clouded out the sun?

Wave to us John, wave to us
with your sweet smile brother.
Your little Scottie who loves only you,
your wife, fierce, intelligent, who
loves only you, look up to heaven,
through their long black bangs.

We are all here below, John, waiting
with outstretched, empty arms.

At the Aquarium

He's a big Palooka, this big Beluga
whiter than Alabaster, but drifting
like a cloud through the tank's blue
waters: unreal, neon
mouthwash blue. Pretty Enoch,
on loan for mating, plays alone,
while his dingy, dishwater consorts,
take notes in the back forty.

"That's were they get the caviar,"
a ditzy tourist announces to all
with sturgeon wit. "No, Enoch
is a mammal," the guide corrects her.
"They give birth to their young
the way we do, though he doesn't
seem too intent on that today."

Sweet Enoch, so sleek and white
sucking a little leaf, the first of autumn,
in and out, blowing deft and gentle
rolling on his back , amusing himself
the way a child will roll a hoop or
run a stick against a fence at summer's end.

Lovely Enoch lost in play, his silly smile,
the black marble of his eye floating by us,
stuck to the glass like sea snails, longing
to join him in that perfect blue solitude.

Armagedon

Hello, hello, we walked
amid this extraordinary flesh

It was perhaps more
extraordinary than yours

flesh you could argue
is flesh.

My sadness.
That I can not now know you.

Yours was not our worry,
We lived in the proverbial garden.

Hello, hello.

Desert Song

No brilliant sea
no robin's egg
no moonlight night
nor morning star.
No longer any
sparkling bells
no flight, no feather
no taste of berry,
touch or silk
nor any sweetness
left in thought or
play of body since
you've taken back
that love which was
the source of joy
like water to the earth,
the very air - only now
this breathless grief
the lifeless sky this
dust and suffocation.

Second Chance Moon

    for Daniella

Her light a silver roadway,
springboard into eternity
across the Black Sea.
Leap - Straight as an arrow
over the planet's edge
into life without you
some beastly future -
comes the end of love,
nothing to be done,
either. Cry all you want,
but don't be a baby about it.
There will be other summers
for saying farewell to a
summer love. There will be
other double moons, winking
at you, flirting across time,
drifting to the other side of dream.
Do not wish upon a falling star,
nor the sailing moon. Look,
look, and take your pleasure
in the night.

Autumn Postcard

The maple burns in silence
The fog horn sings to no one
across the darkAtlantic.
Light dissolves in a
desperate transparency
as the world falls asleep
without you.

If I Were William Meredith

      For Ms. N.I.

If I were William Meredith
I'd have a pretty girl.
She'd kiss me over breakfast
and treat me really swell.

She'd give me a banana,
would ask me how my health is.
And if okay would start perhaps
a little monkey business.

She'd read the morning paper,
would help me start my day with
a little anecdotal piece
of substance and of pith.

But I am not, it seems, alas
the famous William Meredith

In my Tomb Tonight

The dark healer's impossible dream
so, perhaps, slumming
in some other back alley,
trespassing in a family vault
whose name I do not know.

I have been storing up goods
necessary for eternity.
I've placed them in a metal box
safe from mice and worms:
a hundred dollar bill just in
case, your photo
as you were the day at the beach
under the palm trees
staring at the horizon,
my old dog's collar-
for the smell of him,
a blue rock,
some cherry lifesavers.
I've cut one tiny merit badge,
the one for music and left
a ragged hole in the green sash.

I am sitting on the marble floor,
metal box in hand, the cold
spreading through my bones,
certain there will be no sunrise.

In Passing

William can't find his finger nail polish
the anti fungal that he uses every morning
when the directions say use last thing at bed.
"Go to the pharmacy. I can't find it."

Nick's shoes, my leftovers show a threadbare
sole when he crosses his thighs - thighs like
those of Mercury or Apollo. His feet
should be set in silver wings, his beauty
his dignity, deserve more than I can provide.

This lost medicine, this flower of a man
blooming in the garbage - my broken heart.

Which god among you will help me?
Ganesh, Shiva, beloved Saravasti?
Which of you will see these things and
heal a heart too much taken by the world.

A Little Summer Music

Prelude

Just went to the garden
and met a pine tree bigger
than Motzart's father
standing black and enormous
against the early morning sky.
Great garden. My garden. Lucky

I

Suite VI in D Major

    for Christine Gummere

Her left hand flew
through Bach-
a white spider
spinning in a drop
of crystal rain, or
lightly up and down
the tense neck
of her darling
five-stringed cello,
teasing her
unto rapture. Her right,
wind over wheat field,
fierce or gentle
as her sister above,
they signed to each other
over the dark chasm
directly to my heart
fibrillating in the back row.

HE GOES TO PROUST
AND EINSTEIN, LOOKING
AT TIME

   a.

How many centuries now
has this Buddha sat under
the mountain?
How often the electronic bird
chimed to a winter
or a summer lost?

What will it take to
rejuvenate this library?

Work. Love and work.

   b.

A SEASONAL PERSON RETURNS
early June, to his haunt.

JD said first thing.
Your hair is too dark!

Paul was Paul.
Our host a little ill.

Needs a new heart
or something, don't
we all. And home,
alone. Same old place.

c.

Einstein once held

Walter Gezari
in his lap,
revealing the secrets
of the universe
like a unicorn -
local legend.

I am suddenly
rounding the corner,
a red fox is there.
And exactly a year
later, to the day.

I am still, 911,
searching for that fox.
So, these are sacred
shores I live on. Blue
feather drop, or grey.

What sort of brother
shall I be to thee?.

Watching only fox.
Only watching.

Objet Trouvé: In the Faust Lane

For Marie

He, on his car: "It's got Global Satellite Positioning. Tells you where you are at any moment, anywhere in the world. Pretty nifty, huh?"

She, sadly: "Does it tell you where you are in your life?"

No, this the economy model. You'd be wanting the Faustmobile: tells you when to kiss, when to make love, when to pull out: abort, abort. Let's you know how high gold will rise before the price begins to move. Straightens out all the curves: "ATTENTION, the relationship ahead is not suited to your psyche; DANGER, DANGER, DO NOT BACK UP - you are about to blow four years of hard work trying to get things right finally- EXTREME DAMAGE VERY LIKELY. APPROACHING NIRVANA, APPROACHING NIRVANA - enter at your own risk; SLOWER PLEASE, SLOW DOWN: happiness is right around the corner, you are expending too much energy."

This baby has an adjustable suspension system that fills your valleys with lavender and almond blossoms, renders your dreams chocolate. It keeps you firm against the current like a trout smiling up at you from his green bed beneath the glassy waters. It lets you know when to pray, how to die a good death.

Luxurious all right, but it comes with sticker price you'd just as soon not pay, dear.

911 - A Year Later

I lace my jogging shoes a
private protest, to stop
time, to run the exact
three miles I ran last year
as the brilliant sun
stung my eyes and
news of the terror
flooded my headphones.

Some clutched briefcases or
took a friend's hand then to
try the sky, like Icarus,
burned by the sun, shedding
his sad feathers to the white sea.

A thousand Roman paces,
each of my three miles will
sing a thousand lives blown
to the winds that day as
the winds now stir
the crowns of oak trees -
trees stirred by ghosting,
or the winds of war along
the Thames running silver
beside me down to the
nuclear submarines waiting
like patient sharks, silent
at the mouth of the sound.

And in the home stretch
up the last difficult hill
past the country cemetery
where I always pray three
times for the farming
family laid to rest and all
the dear and lately dead
I am dumb, without a prayer,
marking each life, yard by yard,

as I listen to the winds
howling above.

Totem

Tropical fish swim across the coral reef,
the scratched surface of a plastic mug
you drank hot coffee from each morning
As you drove off to your day jobs -

Gardener, stone mason, pizza boy
- the nuts and bolts of American life
tended to by immigrants, illegal like you
to fix their comfort, the obese "lifestyle" -

your favorite mug, despite the faded
underwater glory, washed ghostly now
by a thousand dishwasher nights after a
thousand dusty days of labor.

Here is where you placed your lip to
the steaming cup, driving away fresh,
hopeful at the new day's challenge,
where now I steal a surrogate kiss,

less hopeful, my faded dream like
the murky scene on a plastic cup, once
bright with electric color, bejeweled
vessel for the hand and eye.

To kiss your sweet mug once more.
To send you off smiling at the door
like an eager child the first day of school....
I sit at the window, the afternoon long

drinking from the magic cup,
trying to conjure you back,
a ritual of waiting, to welcome
the yellow bus that never comes home.

Good Friday

Now it is done, now through
the gates of hell, past the pain
and torture, He goes to his tomb,
at some level insensate, at some,
not: What blood remaining sinks
heavily to the stone bier on which
the shell shall lie - he sees this all
he lies in terror, sure he will rise
but afraid too, a purple terror,
for the night, for what has happened,
that day not break or find him
His release. This dark tomb.

Father, you did not tell me of this
strange cessation, my death.

Postcard

Hello Margaret, Hello Bill.
Here's the news from Uncasville.

No Ms. Alice
No Ms. Puskar
I'm Warren Betty
pushing Ishkar.

Friday's come and's
long been gone:
Ms. Torqumeda's
sung no song.

I'm left to hope
by week's beginning
something in D.C.'ll
start spinning

for poetry
and Mr. Bill
in 2004
from Jenkin's Hill.

       Love, R.

September 11, 2004

Fall again, 9/11.
Each night a spider
tries to wall me out
of my studio until I
look him in his ruby eye
and say enough's enough -
he scurries off, decamps
before I find a stick again
to waive him away.

The grapes have fallen like
black tears from the arbor
crushed under foot,
releasing the sun's perfume
before the inevitable rot.

A third hurricane this month
roars into Florida - sweet friends
report the news: <u>news:</u> "Fuck this,
fuck that." Their bright lexicon
dimmed by fear and exhaustion.
New eye, old eye - the waters will
grow aquamarine again, will again.

And you my crusty friend -
growing old as I am growing old
before the flames sent you to sky,
to spirit - You are not here to see it:
What they make of your death,
which way the hurricane will blow.
This is the hard part for me John.
You would have loved to have
been here, this year, and are not.

I pour a little gin on the floor like
wine or blood before setting sail
as if it could assuage your journey
or ours without you now.

Dear Bettie and Charles,

    It is too late to be writing this thank you letter, but perhaps "better late than never" will hold true here. We had such a wonderful reunion in the middle of Charles' beautiful cooking. Really, I was so pleased to see you finally at the end of a busy fall for us all, to reclaim our friendship, and feel the warmth of your household. I came back and made an observation in my journal which I hope you will forgive me if it appears too personal. It recounts a gesture I saw from the corner of my eye which demonstrated love in a very touching way for me. Anyhow, it comes with our love, thanks, and warm best wishes for a pleasant holiday season and continuing good health. We will be thinking of you this winter. Very best to you. Richard and William

Uxorial

Sixty years later,
that long after their
wedding night -
despite her stroke,
despite his occasional
rage at fate,
she knows a gentle caress
behind the ear, as though
she were tracing still
the heart's pleasure
will assuage that red
storm, will bring him back
to the private circle,
the calm center
of their love.

Treat Time

Throughout the day
she could be anywhere- asleep
under the desk, closeted,
atop a pile of shoes, staring up
at the mechanical flamingo,
bobbing slow mo, pink
twinkle lights, hypnotic.

en garde behind the glass door
for geckos who crawl oblivious
the hot day long over David's
naked body like little green fingers
down his torso, up his thighs
caressing the ripe and brilliant youth
turned to marble in the garden.

chewing out the stuffing
from her toy dinosaur -
giving that baby HELL.

But when the fridge door opens,
NORAD goes off and she is
standing at my feet miraculous
like a sweet, bi-located saint
blinking up with jelly-bean eyes,
tiny white teeth smiling,
just in case, daddy, just in case.

Notes on a Hearty Merlot

How the grape is
driven by the sun -
through the vine,
the flowering of her leaves
to the late purple, summer
fulfillment - to take
his spirit as her own.

Homage to Ezra Pound

Today five French boys
stood under the cafe's canopy
after a sudden cloudburst like
pigeons, disinterested
in each other, pecking away at
their cell phones, cigarettes.

Each had a rainbow around his neck
Each had hair blacker than night.

When I was a child I was told that
if I put salt on a bird's tail he could not
fly and I might take him home with me.

I remember - four years old - chasing
and chasing while the adults sat
laughing at the dining room table.

I watch myself now,
alone in the café
as these young beauties
flutter each on his way
into the afternoon sunshine.

At the Opera

      After William Meredith

Everything's sad.
Everyone's mad.

Oxymoronic

 For he's a jolly Othello......
And nobody else shall die.

The Stewardess Sizes Up Herbert

"Mr. Von Karien,

you have a very large carry-on."

FAREWELL SUPERMAN

For Helen and Franklin Reeve

We thought your youth would never end.
Faster than a speeding bullet, able to leap
the tallest building in a single bound -
brought low by a simple hurdle,
a stupid hangnail of fate, like an arrow
piercing the heel of an unsuspecting hero.

The tallest buildings have collapsed
in flame, green as Kryptonite.
Your great heart has burst,
your radiant smile is extinguished.

You've taken that final leap
beyond the stars we all
must one day make, beyond
space and time to the
mystery of eternity.

Like children, we pick up
your cape and try it on for size,
dreaming of a big boy's muscles,
becoming the gentleman
mama wants us to be,
dropping softly to the ground
with a beautiful girl in our arms,
her face transparent with love.

The terrible weight has lifted.
The earth falls into shadow,
a brief eclipse of the sun
as you make your way back home.

Housekeeping

That time of year again:
The sky goes grey, the leaves have
been blown away, it begins to
feel like snow. Time once again
for the killing fields.

Ever so carefully - these things
could break your finger - you
pull back the metal bar, balance
a piece of cheese, affix the trigger
delicate as lovers's whisper, and
slide the traps, armed claymores,
across the kitchen counter:
terrifying, such trapped energy
in such a tiny machine. It's there
all night long, like nightmare.

The bar will come thwacking down
out of nowhere as the mouse,
oblivious, takes his last supper,
will cut him in half like a
Jihadi's sword, take him by
surprise, like a simple lab report
announcing you are HIV positive,
like the Mack truck coming round
the bend as you shoo away a
summer bee for just the last
distracting moment, or gaze
out your window as the plane,
as in a dream, comes smashing
through your office in flame.

How did the ancient Greeks have it:
we are to the gods like flies to boys
who tear off wings and smear them out,
out only perhaps of juvenile boredom.

Still, the cupboards are a riot of
shredded flour sacks, and ruined
cereals. Even the labels have been
eaten off the dog's food - little
piles of mouse turds cover the dishes
and line the wine glasses in just the
few short weeks I've been away.

Would a Buddhist simply share his fare
and go down together, plague be damned.

Each morning, I'll lift the metal bar
which has come so mercifully swift
avoiding the tiny black eyes, so sweet,
as though they could blink away their
surprise and scurry back to the nest.

I'll take no pleasure in the one caught
only by the shoulder, dragging the trap
backward against all odds till I release
him to the toilet's depths. I'll take
no pleasure knowing how to bait
the trap, or fix a deer in the cross hairs,
or watch my countrymen destroy a city
as though it were a rat's nest, as though
the dark-eyed children were but mice
caught by accident in the crossfire.

I'll have my coffee and ponder my talent
for violence, an ape scratching his head,
reaching for a banana from the pretty girl
who comes each morning to clean his cage.

Cat Burglary: on the loss of the Vaptsarov Medal

For Roger and Sara

The cat lies curled into a great ball
like a party boss sleeping off
too much rakia at the summer
politburo picnic. This is one fat
cat - she keeps her counsel,
dreams, who knows what silent
terrors on mouse or sparrow.

She's tired herself out,
toying with the shining lozenge:
heroic Nikola hung on a golden chain,
rattling so seductively in the
little black jewelry box coffin
she's pilfered from our luggage
the way, at death, they stole
your image for public consumption.

Dudley Do Right, Balkan Style
Granite jaw, hair, a black forest,
pure eyes, straight as steel
railway ties into the future
Soap opera beautiful,
paradigm of youth
harnessed like a work horse,
one man political nag
to pull the party's troika
round and round the town square.
Where has she buried you Nikola?
sing to us from your green hiding place.
Rise like a sunflower in the fields of Bulgaria
and show us your shining face once again.

Death of a Pope: 4/7/05

The white dove flies up
announcing the release of
your spirit to the world.
Millions file by your body
gravity taking hold, plum
bruises singing through your
make up now - you would be
buried in the earth, the very
world your marble sepulcher.

In this season of death
this eternal Easter it seems
with Terry Shiavo consuming
the houses of government, the
media, the questions-
who loves, who is cruel,
what is life or death after all,
you rally the faithful.

And I am left alone again
dreaming of John XXIII
the hope of my youth,
the good grandfather who
slips you a candy, puts you
on his lap, forgives you, and
loves you. So wrong, so wrong
you want to say. Now Tucker
calls to say that Jane too is dead.
You think of your own mother
alone in her apartment, wondering
what day it is and calling the girl
at Wal-Mart to find out what day it is.

Well, we wish his spirit well,
of course. Well, he is man, after all,

and also John Paul the Great.
But why this terrible loneliness
why so feeling at odds with
all the millions, the YOUNG
millions, for whom the
sepulcher is a sweet
confirmation, an alabaster love,
or a kind of electric plasma
engulfing the planet, mysterious
as the internet, the stigmata,
the perfume of roses.

Rest in peace father,
this my prayer, and I
will try to do the same
and keep the faith.

Portraits

"And now, a moment of silence for those who have recently died in Iraq whose images we present as they become available to us."
Jim Lerher

The commentator, old now,

eyes black buttons of surprise
with bags below bigger than my own,
bigger than Bill Clinton's even,
little seas of flesh he refuses to cut out,
anymore than the portraits of the dead
that grace the last moments of
his newscast, theirlives.

The very young dead, whose eyes
are sometimes troubled too -
unsure, guilty at times with the
sins of youth, indecision or fear
as the world opens to them.

But free eyes mostly, eyes
where the whites have not gone
rheumy, eyes that laugh into
a girlfriend's camera, eyes that
fix the photographer with a
steely blue "yes, I am, yes I will," or
sometimes petulant eyes: "won't you?
Didn't you, won't you please, just
one more chance?" And the answer is no.

The commentator knows the answer
is never more. The unblinking young
dead turn his old eyes red, his eyes
cloud with tears and blur his vision
like the final image of a soldier picking
up his helmet and walking into the sun
that closes the Nightly News Hour.

High Style at J.C. Pennay's

"I can always sell shoes at J.C. Penny's,"
I sometimes tell the family when speaking of
my uncertain future. Today, I'm not so sure.

The phone wakes me from a Sunday afternoon nap
as I lay fitful, sweated, at the mercy of dark dreams,
doing my psyche's laundry.

"Hello, Reechard, I got da shoe for you,"
the clerk from Penny's calls as I struggle back into
myself from some stranger's dingy Laundromat.
The missing sandal, size twelve, from the last pair
of a discontinued style for which I would have gladly
paid twice as much, all leather, slit on the side and
slung at the heel, square-toed like little shovels,
kind of gay, a little risqué, a shoe Louis XVI
would have been proud to wear has at last been found!

Like Ponce de Leon or Mercury I stood at the cash register
elbowing my way in with the others yesterday thinking this
shoe will restore my youth, will lift my fallen arches and
cure my tingly, suffocating toes. Shoes wide enough to
accommodate feet which have run too many marathons and
now begin to swell by the end of the day I notice,
sad as a mother who first sees her son's hair has begun to turn
to grey: lacrimae raerum, but worse. One's gone missing,
and it's no deal unless I somehow loose a foot in the near future.
I carry my black heart home in an empty shoe box, certain
the clerk will never call me back, as promised, if he finds it.

I was one of the flood sticking shoes in his face all day Saturday
demanding this size or that, the right color, the right price.

"I have a 3 and a 4, no 3 and a half, madame," he says,
with equanimity and the memory of a late model computer
to the teenage mother. How can he keep the leather tide
which threatens to break like a Tsunami from behind

the storeroom curtain all inventoried in his mind? And
why can't he remember the single shoe that troubles
my imagination like the proverbial pea hidden under the
mattress of a peevish princess. There he stood in his
ridiculous outfit, some private uniform he dreamed up,
cuffs and collar striped in blue to match his shirt and
matching pocket scarf. Sapphire cuff links the size of grapes,
remembered perhaps from his boyhood in Beirut in the 60's,
handling each customer with the dignity of a visiting sheik,
the Minister of Culture, a soap opera star in some Arab version
of Days of our Lives. Each day of his life, 9-5 at Penny's,
the Minister of Culture to the American hordes in cut offs
and flip flops in a hurry and looking for a bargain.

"Have a nice day," I said, with the searing irony of a frustrated
telemarketer when he couldn't give me the shoe I wanted.

I'd have probably said, "You can't always get what you want, Sir,
Mick Jagger" and not promised to call back. So, clever these Arabs:
"Reechard, I got da shoe for you." And I'm out of a job and
wondering where I might take him for a strong mint tea and
Ramadan cookies just by way of saying merci.

The lone swan

makes his radiant way
on a ribbon of liquid light that
mirrors the sky's proud flag,
ablaze in red and gold and lavender.

Such a brave white chest
gliding effortlessly
on the water, concealing
the great paddles pulling
against the current below.

Where is he going in the
fading light? Where is
his legendary mate? Not even
his reflection for comfort,
oblivious to his beauty.

Tonight no foxes will ruin his nest
no hunter trespass in his sleep.
Tonight he will climb the ladder
of light cast across the water
to lay his breast against the moon
and wrap his darling in his wings
so love and dream will blanket
the world in their sweet shadow.

Thank You Note to John Rigo

9/11/06

Hi John,

    Here I am five years later. I wave to you from the other side of time - you there now, eternal, and me plodding along, thinking if I wasn't good at 16, I might at least try to be okay at 60.
    Different strange events John. Daily, a hundred dead in Iraq. They wave your memory like a tattered flag over Iowa Jima, John. The Crocodile Hunter, like Ahab, skewered into the dark by some gangster from the deep. And me too John, blooming once again from the evil seed, trusting to my young gardener and the over reaching God who I pray holds you in his sweet hand as well.
    Tonight I sang with the chorus in a Brahms Requiem- Candles and silence after 911. I spoke your name to the assembly. The music was extremely intricate, I came in too late for the very last note. There I was, naked, in the pew.
    I seem to be a baritone these days. I take Viagra on occasion. My hair is the color of straw again. But one of the things I can be glad for is you - template of youth, a man to measure yourself by, keeping perspective as you grow and train and live your present life.

Preparing for Death

If you look closely
You'll meet her shy,
Mongolian eyes.
Take the time,
she will delight you.

Pay off all the bills, yes,
but find a way to keep my love
alive, should he despair.

Mother, perhaps, will be
inconsolable, perhaps not.
She goes her own way,
has taught me the value in this:
If I stood on a ledge, the fire
licking at my back, she would
surely say, "Jump!"

Please erase the wrong ideas
I have espoused. Burn or otherwise
destroy them as they were a kind
of self betrayal. Don't let me

Suffer, if death is imminent or
inevitable with suffering.

The future will take care of itself,
I can't say what my passing will mean,
but for those I love I wish only not
to be a burden in death, wish only
that some good, some pleasure
will have come to them
along the course of my life.

The thought that you will listen
to this request consoles me as

I prepare to face the unknown
and trust my life to
God and other hands.

The Speech Therapist Makes a House Call

Dr. Schnur arrives, brown tie
brown shoes, brown briefcase.
"Good morning you," his patient
says back as they begin the
morning session, how to talk,
how to light the mind's dark labyrinth
where language has gone missing,
how to frame experience in concepts,
there's a funny word, "what is
concept, I don't understand."

I listen to them work as I do
the dishes below. Two old men
talking about the war, sweet
with each other over tongue
depressors, and exercises -
say "ah, ah." Who can park
in private parking? What is
the boy doing in this photo?
Tell me your name again please.

How many decades has Dr. Schnur
dressed in his brown uniform and
packed his brown briefcase to start
the day, to take someone's hand
and make baby steps toward speech.
He could have retired years ago but
why? Why miss the chance to w
walk with a friend as the air
sharpens and color bleeds into the
fall foliage. Soon enough winter,
and angels do not shed theirwings.

In Vino Veritas

Would I were
a Juno Merlot:
"Brave, beautifully
balanced, complex
yet approachable."
Ah, that'd be me,
mamma's dream,
pride of Johannesburg,
paragon of vintners
aged to perfection.

 But I alas, good
tippler that I am
am often far from
balanced, take
courage in a glass
of stout, will buy a
round for anyone
about the bar who
smiles my way,
skindeep's about
my depth.

Your garden variety oenophile,
more Thunderbird or Ripple
than Johannes Burgundy Juno,
a spirit a great deal easier
to drink than imitate.

Colony Collapse
Disorder*

Karl Rove lies hidden ,
sheltered like the Queen
by lady workers and male drones
in the center of the hive.

In the orchards of America
almond blossom and cherry
drift listless in the breeze
no birds or bees to play matchmaker,
move indolent stamen and pistil
to seed and fruit and blossom again:
Colony Collapse Disorder
on a national scale.

"Let them eat pollen,"
the queen opines
drifting into sleep
while in the ancient valley
of Tigris and Euphrates -
biblical Eden where life began -
flowers bleed and the winds
keen with the last cries of
the tortured dead.

The earth spins, the hive dreams
and spirits float in the blue air
like the delicate shells of summer bees.

*Recently reported epidemic among American bees.

A Graduate of York Catholic High School
Takes the Ten Minute Quiz Late at Night.

10 Things Every High School Graduate Should Know

(http://access.nscpcdn.com/cp/fte/sciencequestions/i/sciencequestions135.jpg)

What is one science question every high school graduate should be able to answer?" That's the question a team of Nobel laureates, science teachers and writers and leading scientists were asked, and the results of their answers is a 10-question science quiz you should be able to pass with flying colors if you have a high school diploma.

Andrea L. Gawrylewski, a reporter with the Columbia News Service, assembled this quiz that is probably more difficult than you're anticipating. Even your teenager might not be able to help you. Why? The National Center for Education Statistics reports that only 60 percent of high school students complete a general biology class, 40 percent complete a general chemistry test and just 27 percent complete a physics class. And even if you took all three in high school, you probably don't remember all the details.

Here are 10 science questions every high school graduate should know:

What percentage of the earth is covered by water?
Answer: About 71 percent of the earth's surface is covered by water.
--Submitted by Robert Gagosian, Woods Hole Oceanographic Institute

R: Easy. Most of it. And its tides pull us from within when there is a full moon. We remember water from our time in the womb too, when we first developed consciousness. And there is a lot down there we don't understand or know about either. Which is why Hollywood makes a mint on films like JAWS, or Melville could contemplate the great white beast below, death, fate, sin, with not a chance whatsoever for resurrection.

What sorts of signals does the brain use to communicate sensations, thoughts and actions?
Answer: The single cells in the brain communicate through electrical and chemical signals.

--Submitted by Torsten Weisel, Rockefeller Institute, New York

R. Answer: chemicals first, electro chemical stimulation on a neuron: vision. But also, faith messages, astro projectional contact, a kind of merging into this neurological gel surrounding the earth, or a transcendent concept involving love, going beyond time, time pushing matter into the future, gravity on the remote side as a result. This will be come clearer in the future.

Did dinosaurs and humans ever exist at the same time?

Answer: No. Dinosaurs went extinct at the end of the Cretaceous period, 65 million years ago. Modern humans did not appear until around 200,000 years ago.
--Submitted by Andrew C. Revkin, New York Times Science Reporter

R. Only in the imagination of some wacked out, Bible-belted mentality of some righteous fundamentalist from the swamps. Of course, time machines can correct bigotry as well as history, so let's hope Jules Verne has hit on something.

What is Darwin's theory of the origin of species?
Answer: Darwin's theory of species origination says that natural selection chooses organisms that possess variable and heritable traits and that are best suited for their environments.
--Submitted by Jonathan Weiner, 1995 Pulitzer Prize-Winning Author

R. We're the next step in evolution after homo hominis or whatever the next in the line is. We started as chemical bonding then got complex, developed brains, and somehow got electrocuted with intelligence and self awareness. The theory seems sound but doesn't account for everything, by a long shot.

Why does a year consist of 365 days and a day of 24 hours?
Answer: A year, 365 days, is the time it takes for the Earth to travel around the Sun. A day, 24 hours, is the time it takes for the Earth to spin around once on its axis.
--Submitted by Leslie Sage, Nature Magazine

R. A convenience to make our clocks run. Why not think in terms of months or years, or moon cycles. Astronomers needed a little wiggle room, as do astrologers.

Why is the sky blue?
Answer: Solar radiation sunlight is scattered across the atmosphere by a process called diffused sky radiation. The sky is blue because much more short-wave radiation--blue light--is scattered across the sky than long-wave radiation—red light.
--Submitted by Roy Glauber, 2005 Nobel Prize Winner; Harvard University

R. Dust eats red light and ignores blue? To keep us happy?

What causes a rainbow?
Answer: Rainbows can be seen when there are water droplets in the air and the sun is shining. Sunlight, which contains all colors, is refracted, or bent, off the droplets at different angles, splitting into its different colors of red, orange, yellow, green, blue, indigo and violet.
--Submitted by Kim Kastens, Columbia University

R. Ibid. Nature wishes to keep us happy, and demonstrate the variations that can be produces when light is fractured. Which is why homosexuals have taken it as a symbol of beauty in nature.

What is it that makes diseases caused by viruses and bacteria hard to treat?
Answer: Influenza viruses and others continually change over time, usually by mutation. This change enables the virus to evade the immune system of its host so that people are susceptible to influenza virus infection throughout their lives. Bacteria mutate in the same way and can also become resistant if over treated with antibiotics.

--Submitted by Helle Gawrylewski, Johnson & Johnson

R: As opposed to what other sorts of diseases, Mr. Ms.? Gawrylewski. The question seems to cover the gamut. I think he wants to stress viruses such as HIV. We need to cover the cells with a kind of teflon so they don't attract and hold such viruses. And also, generally, people can't afford the medicine often to cure these diseases and they spread and people die.

How old are the oldest fossils on earth?
Answer: About 3.8 billion years; they're bacteria-like organisms.
--Submitted by Paul Nurse, 2001 Nobel Prize Winner; Rockefeller Institute

R: Old as the hills (Depending on the hill you find them in.)

Why do we put salt on sidewalks when it snows?
Answer: Adding salt to snow or ice increases the number of molecules on the ground surface and makes it harder for the water to freeze. Salt can lower freezing temperatures on sidewalks to 15 degrees from 32 degrees.
--Submitted by Arthur Knudsen, Bridgeton, N.J., Schools

Source: The Columbia News Service

So we don't break our neck, dummy.

<script></script><NOSCRIPT><A HREF="http://servedby.advertising.com/click/site=0000714488/mnum=000 0446838/optn=64?trg=http://ad.doubleclick.net/jump/N3989.aol.com/B2140 215.23;abr=!ie4;abr=!ie5;sz=160x600;ord=6430434656?"><IMG SRC="http://ad.doubleclick.net/ad/N3989.aol.com/B2140215.23;abr=!ie4;ab r=!ie5;sz=160x600;ord=6430434656?" BORDER=0 WIDTH=160
HEIGHT=600 ALT="Click Here"></a></noscript>
 <http://access.nscpcdn.com/g/i/dot_D2C9AB.gif>
<http://access.nscpcdn.com/g/i/logo_ns40.gif> Copyright © 2007 Netscape Communications Corporation. All rights reserved.

Poems from LEGACY, elegiac songs
distributed privately after the death of William Meredith

I

Memorial Day, 2007

I sit like a God
in the hospital penthouse
watching the crows
on the lower roof top
taking their supper -
old french fries, pilfered
from a dumpster, AC run off,
and stagnant rainwater.

All the bright day long,
ferries glide back and forth
to the islands. The nation
takes its pleasures: burgers
and chicken on the grill,
long walks, hand in hand,
a game of golf or tennis,
and remember a little
their dead. I sit alone with
my dying lover contemplating
hospice decisions, what to hold
what to give, like a Greek boy
whose need to rip the wings from flies
can not fully be explained.

II
Death and Taxes
two sure things,
both a certainty tonight.

April 15 has come and gone,
the IRS will surely call.
And as my darling lies sleeping
he turns his head from
time to time to the electrical storm
lighting up his dreams:

"You sulphurous and thought-executing fires,
Vaunt couriers of oak-cleaving thunderbolts,
Singe my white head! And thou, all shaking
              Thunder,
Strike flat the thick rotundity o' the world!"
Down the hall, a man heaves and
heaves, nothing left, can not empty
himself into the night. As I keep late watch
once again: time it seems, no longer on our side.

A dark figure, stands at the door,
his hand outstretched. "Pay up,
young Yankee, come along.
And you may yet get out alive."

III

Evensong

This bronze angel against the grey of evening,
wreaths in hand, like tambourines to celebrate
your own genius, that balance, that talent
to stand on a ball fire, grow trees,
love profoundly, inspire: model of
civility, the ultimate good guy.

Now your blue eyes grow grey
with the fading of the light.
You breathe steadily into the blue
oxygen mask, preparing for lift off.
What adventure awaits you? This
private mission we all must undertake.
Do I ask you to look out for me from
the stars as you have done all these years?
I know you will, I know I needn't ask.
I'll keep the angel though,
I'll hold her hostage to keep
your memory safe here on earth
where we have known you
and will love you
until it is time
myself to take flight.

IV

In Memoriam, May 30, 2007

The moon was full, the evening cool,
a perfect night for dying. We packed up
our room and had Irish whiskey with friends
into the night. I know that was the last time I
will ever see you in life, growing cold under
my touch. I kissed your lips, made
the fish "o" they had become and took in
from your lungs the last breath. And I guess,
gave you mine. And your words come back:

"I think dear one that one day I'll fall off this
galaxy, leaving husk and canvas behind, the
loneliness I'll take with me made whole,
myself made whole, by what we've said

in these knocking moments, oh,
and keeping, as hearts keep
(husks and canvas being little abandoned houses),
and going away so."

And the loneliness I am left with is made whole
too my dear, by what we've said and been for
each other all these long years. But, oh, oh,
I seem already to be lost in the cold skin
of the globe, aching for the moon.

V

Sentimental Reveille

Each day begins the same:
"Where are you my love?"
The terrible fact - you are no more,
are not lying still asleep beside me,
not the sweet echo, as I call the dog
to join us in bed to lick your nose,
to start the day, each startling
morning now without you.

She cocks her head
and licks instead my tears.

A penguin, a white wolf
take shape in the crumpled
tissues on the night stand,
affirm the dull irony:
When the sun pours into my sleep
And I first open my eyes, you
are never to be seen again,
but in dream.

Legacy

People loved your blue eyes
your crooked smile. The nurses
puzzled over your biceps, rock
hard from transplanting trees.

These were the spirit's tools -
love, compassion, strength
and courage becoming flesh.

As a man will inherit a strong back
blond hair, or a gentle disposition,
The end to grief may lie within.

A private transformation:
To let your spirit work in me
so that if I am kind for your sake,
in your memory, if I remember
how sweetly you dealt with others
and model myself on that civility,
if I stand against injustice, bigotry
or hatred as you did, then your life
goes on in me, your death no longer
meaningless, your death no longer
death, at least while I live or
this poem, the well will be
replenished, my small steps join
the tribe's slow progress.

Homework

The manuals describe
four responses to tragedy:

Stoicism
Martyrdom
Suicide
Transformation

Who wouldn't go for
door number four?

"Good memories
pushing us
forward."

"All life is on loan."

"The demons of self-pity
and discouragement drag
us into darkness."

All true, all true.
But he will never come back
nor I, nor you.

I lay the book aside
and weep.

Adrift

Afraid I may actually die
of a broken heart, I visit
the local ER for an EKG,
CPK levels for an old MI,
an MRI, a CT or
PET scan:
an alphabet soup when you're
out of sorts body and soul,
some chicken broth when
you're feeling chicken, a little
TLC, the occasional PDA.

Decisiveness is manliness as
Marie Antoinette discovered
with the price of her head, but
I'm a Jackson Pollack portrait
of indecision, a textbook mess.

"Get back, get back, get back
to where you want to belong,"
as the Beatles sang. Cher should
stomp into my kitchen and
slap me up the side of my head:
"Snap out of it!" But how to get
your mojo back?

"Are you happy," I asked the
peanut princess who floated
up to William in his wheel chair
as we strolled one evening at
flamingo hour in West Palm Beach.
"What's not to like," said the young
divorcee, sipping her mojito martini.

"I live in this palace, I shop every day.
Look at this belt," she said, twirling
around her tight little blue-jeaned butt.
"It cost two thousand dollars!"
"But are you lonely," I ask.

"I've got 'Sir lance a lot'," she laughs,
her electric charger. She's not interested
in a toy boy. She's after the old boy I've
bailed out of the nursing home. It's
his eyes and beautiful smile she's after
that no longer ever will light my life again
as pink clouds take flight in the evening sky.

Anecdotal

One evening
as he lay dying
he begged me
not to go.

The dog needed tending,
but he grabbed my hand
with a desperation
I'd never seen in him.

I stayed until the
morphine calmed him
and came back after.

But the thought of his
needing me so
will break my heart
until one day we
rest for ever
together again.

Pathetic Fallacy

Rain at last this summer morning
when day after day the relentless sun
burned the land, a blanket of heat
heavy as grief, the sweltering dream
I've lived in since your death.

Each morning the particulars
overwhelm me, each night
I take your ghost to bed.

I wear a sunburst on my shoulder,
you, a crescent moon and star -
cliché symbols the tattoo artist
thought cute in two guys 60 and 88.

I burn on alone, out of balance
as cardinals play in the summer rain.

"He'll have to live with it," the doctor said
when I asked for something to relieve your
nightmares. "No, no. No antibiotics
for the swollen eye. The eye drops will do."

I'd like to carve his words into the sky,
write them on the walls with my blood.
But the world I guess has enough proof
of man's potential for cruelty.

I stare at the small bottle on my desk:
Akwa Tears, 15 ml, disp: 05/25/07.
The bottle is almost full, but
your eyes are closed forever now,
and I have no need of artificial tears.

After the Rain

For decades I tended to
the details of your life:
bathing, cooking,
filling the pill box
doing the laundry -
soup to nuts.

Tonight, at my leisure
I sit alone on the point
in awe as the Thames dissolves
into a Chinese landscape,
the delicate fog, a grey curtain
erasing the horizon
obscuring the far river bank.

A lone swan glides by me
as if to ask my business
then tucks his head into
his beautiful chest to rest.

What in God's name
ever made me think
it would be easier
when you were gone?

The Deer are after the Apples Again

taking their summer pleasure.
They graze beneath the tree outside
my window as though they lived
in a children's petting zoo.

I watch them as I frame
a favorite photo: It's 4:00 a.m.,

I've dressed you in a woolen cap
and heavy parka for the early
morning ride to surgery. No
complaint about the hour, no
grievance with the surgeon,
you smile a cautious smile
as if to show me how a man
should face his death if a man.

The cardinals are stripping
the gooseberry bush as I slide
the image of courage under glass.
It's time to get to work!

The deer are after the apples again.
But how shall we live in the winter?
Counsel

"Crash and burn," anxious pilots
called to each other at take off
during the war, the way actors
bid each other break a leg
on opening night. Well,
it seems our luck's run out.

86

At last it seems you have spiraled
down in flame without escape.
I've made a little altar for your dear
ashes till we return them
to earth: a photo from the garden,
a wilted rose from the funeral,
an icon of the Blessed Mother.

Friends write and tell me
you stayed on among the stars
like Venus rising in the velvet
blue of summer. I search the sky
looking for you among the fine
needles which pierce the dark.

But you are nowhere to be found,
are lost to me in their cold
brilliance, the infinite sea of light.

This story will not end in joy,
nomatter what they say.

Apology

Three years after your husband
jumped from the 102nd floor,
flames licking his heels, I told you
"Enough Betsy, it's time to move on."

I meant it in friendship, with love:
I felt sorry for your pain, wanted
to talk of something other than death
when I got your late-night phone calls.

Well-meaning friends will no doubt
soon hand me back my own words.
"It will take time," they say,
"you will be okay with time."

What is time supposed to do for me,
I wonder? Is it simply a matter of
forgetting you, is that what's expected?
Cleaning the closets of all your hats
and coats and shoes? Putting your photos
into a drawer, your ashes into the vault.

I insist on this pain if letting you drift
into the past is the price I must pay for
happiness. The lessons we learn in life!
How glib you must have thought me
Betsy, when I played Dutch Uncle
and wrapped my tired cliché about
the granite reality of your grief.

Vin Triste

Daisy was first a baby on this deck,
high over the river. Baby Daisy walked
up to the bucket candles and the light
flickered into her dark eyes like
the magic in the caves of Lascaux.
She never burned her nose, never
caught her chocolate fur on fire. She
was born for this place, claimed it as
her own. And now I walk to the
river, the way we used to do, glass
in hand to watch the fading light of day.

There, swans dot the far bank like
flecks of cotton. Her eyes gone opal
with age, she can not see them, she
bumps into logs and strays from the path.
The mourning doves begin their low, soft
keening. She sits beside me, silky under
my hand, like a weary Oedipus, trying
to understand, searching the river for
you. Neither of us speaks.

I almost can not bear how vision
has taken on the weight of gravity,
every image on the retina a stone,
that simple blade of river grass
pushing through the rock, a sign of
what I mustaccomplish,
the little dog's blind vigil, true
as the dogs guarding the sleep
of a dead crusader's tomb, the
incriminating light itself, showing

me how often I took your presence
for granted, and simply didn't speak.

"We kept warm together
in cycles of our own turning,"
you wrote once, as the planet
tilted north again. And yes, we did.
You and me and Daisy sat on
the river in firelight, part of it all,
not perfection, but we had those
moments when we were as
much a part of the landscape
as the great oaks holding the river
bank from melting into the ocean

I tip my glass and let the red wine
nourish the earth and your spirit,
a custom from our adopted homeland,
in hopes, that perhaps, it will save us,
and in gratitude.

Gardening

Sunday morning I wake to the sound
of Richie's backhoe extracting the dead
cherry tree that bit like a rotten tooth
into the horizon all winter long,
victim of the evil honeysuckle, your
arch enemy, the 60 years you lived here.

Daisy jumps and barks in the freshly
plowed earth which matches her color
exactly, the excitement of a child on
moving day, a much better game than
licking my nose to rouse me out of bed.

"Coffee, with only cream," Richie calls
from the tractor's cabin and waves,
proud of his neighborly gesture.

"William would have loved
doctoring the trees like this," I tell him,
memory creeping like honeysuckle,
about to choke my heart again, despite
the promise of the freshly tilled earth.

"Ah, he's here all right. He's pruning
over in the secret garden," Richie says,
revving up his engine, blowing off a little
black smoke. A slight breeze rises from
nowhere, but the day will be blistering.

Maybe, Richie. Maybe he is.

Aubade

The gentle deer, lifts one leg
then another, grazing at sunrise
like a puppet on strings. You
could weep for the delicate,
impossible tendons on which
it moves: a cloud, a sunflower
drawn to the sun's slow course.

A humming bird drinks
the hollyhock fountain,
miraculous, in mid-air,
tiny summer rainbow.

If you listen carefully,
you can hear the trees
sing their green joy.

How can I bear this
without you?

Quandary

There is a boy with sandy red hair
making love to me who shoos away
a competitor and suggests that we
drink each other's blood and flesh.

I am driving with people I don't like.
When we get to the end of the road,
the road leads into the ocean, all
is blue water and it is filling the car.
There is no escape and I can not wake.

When you were alive you would have
shaken me and made it clear, even
without words that it was a bad dream,
that I was loved, that I was safe
in the real world of your smile and arms.

What am I to do with no one now
to rouse me from nightmare?

Moot Epiphany

The "grief counselor" is smart
and sweet – Jesus sandals and
a pony tail. Jungian, I suspect.

He says we are a true rarity,
more than simply mates.
Two souls that have intertwined,
whose beings have merged and
depend so totally on each the other,
we are one person. My ego flickers
somewhere below consciousness
like a low-battery alarm.

"This is not pathology," he says,
"It can even be seen as something
very glorious. You have taken a
different road, the road less traveled.
But now you see the enormous
price you must pay for who you are."

He hands me my head and
half of my heart with a gentle smile
as I close the office door behind me.

After Berry Picking

The cardinals are pissed,
the blue jays on strike.
The mocking birds, speechless,
the humming birds grounded.
Even the bees are a buzz.

I've come like Katrina
to ravish the gooseberry,
thorns and twigs my
late night legacy.

What could I do? Every day
I passed by the rare jewels,
garnet and jade, no security
in sight, ready for the picking.

I slipped on Pink Floyd for a
little distraction, fired up the
barbeque as a smoke screen.

Tonight I'll get out Fannie Farmer
and breakfast on jam and crumpets.
Sorry boys, that's life. I'm a little
angry myself of late. Go make whoopee
with some grey thing in the bushes.

Procrastination

Now comes a gentle rain,
drawn like a curtain across
the dusty plot I'd thought
to seed and lime and turn to lawn.
Another missed chance, failed chore:

The gooseberries languish
in the dark fridge like a
saintly host waiting to
sacrifice themselves in a
pot of boiling sugar.

The condolence letters
throb on my desk, the bills
cry out for answer.

The ominous engine light
I've been ignoring all week
burns like a third eye, while I
stare out through the languid rain
in useless, luxurious freedom.

Night Flower

Frangipani blossoms fall and melt
like lemon creamsicles on the sidewalk
as Daisy and I retrace your steps
on the little runway to the corner -
all you could manage at the end -
but, a stretch you insisted on trying
every flamingo evening
before the dark descended.

Each night now I float a single,
rescued blossom in a golden cup
beside your ashes - the petal's delicate
flesh, so ripe, so delicious looking
feeding your spirit's memory:
how secretly you admired my efforts
to keep death at bay, our private
mutual enterprise - love informing joy.

But by morning, the blossom
curls in corruption, ominous rust
at the petal's fragile edge, to mirror
our dissolved partnership.

I begin another day, navigating
the murky waters without you.
What a world now - astonishing,
how beauty fades without you.

Another February 14th

Last year candy stripers
came to serenade you.
There was a heart-shaped
cake, the day was pink.
You sat alone, powdered
and fresh in your wheel chair
and when you saw me
coming down the hall,
burst open like the sun.

Each of us was saved.

Now, I measure my life
in holidays without you.
Time and distance are
not working, your death
isa great stone within me.

Who will I love,
who will I everlove?

IDLING ATRIVERRUN

Board Meeting

Odd to wake thinking of time
and electricity at once - how
each is a mystery common
as the air we breathe,
or the cliche explanation of God:
like the invisible hand
caressing a field of wheat,
His existence no less "real"
if seen with the eyes of faith.

Or love. Sweet Daisy jumps
onto your side of the bed,
gone now nearly a year, and
still can not stop shaking for
missing you.

You, who survives in my daily rituals, the
years of friendship you gave students,
the threads of wisdom that tie you
to our history and our future.

So, later today I'll teleconference with friends
and gather a board of directors:
Bill and Betsy, Marilyn and Nancy,
Grace and Daniel, Laurie and Tim,
Michael and maybe Charlie.
All on one line, mirabile dictu,
another mystery. All of us circling about,
out in the aether there somewhere - maybe
you'll join us honey, why not -
gathering to create something electric,
something that will stand up to time,
driven by love and memory.

Café Bistro, Johan Strauss, Vienna

Arab matrons drift like designer
crows through the airport lobby,
wheel their young through duty
free, the Caviar House, to stock
the nest in Riyadh or Bahrain.

Scarlet flight attendants flutter
their serious way to the gate, a
flock of cardinals on a mission.

Pilots and navigators strut like so
many cocky blue jays on the terrace.

And at the Café Bistro, Turkey-necked
Viennese gobble down Berner Würstel,
Brombeerschinitte and hot chocolate
waiting to be called to heaven.

I sit like an alley cat, taking it in
by the hour without you, here
where only months ago, we sat,
drank beer, checked passports -
jolly colleagues in the aviary,
the blue air infinite, like life itself.

William's Notion of Courage, 1945

Being afraid doesn't matter.
Doing what must be done matters.
And not making too much of it
along the way.

Grey Humor Before Surgery

William would always say
when he knew that something
was out of order, or that death
was knocking at his door:

"Funny, isn't it?"

And would administer that half
smile, but a smile, to make you
love him, and keep it real
more or less.

Pirate's Ball

The moon hangs like a bucket
on the black belly of night
half full of light and my blood.

The pirates are counting their gold
and drinking wine. Hams glisten
on the hearth and the air fills with
the scent of sweet meats. A great
skull clouds the sky and smiles
over the frozen earth. Fox

barks out the invitation and a
warning that soon in the forest
on the hill, the pirates will revel:
"Hold onto your wallets, lock up
your zipper and your heart. Come
be kissed by a pirate if you dare."

Ричард Хартайс

ПЛЕНЕР

По друмите от град на град
пътуващ трубадур, на амулет подобен,
приятели художници следя виденията
им наяве
в масло и акварел,
и техните мечти – неповторими
подобно на душите им
след вино, ракия или изворна вода.

"Езикът ни", бе казал майсторът,
"наподобява акварел,
изтлява твърде бързо.
Необходимо е да знаеш онова,
което търсиш, да го хванеш мигом.
Защото, рано или късно
сълзите всичко разводняват –
и твоите и на другите сълзите.
Контрастите се гонят неотстъпно
един след друг, ала не бива
да им уйдисваме. Чрез тях
по-ясно виждаме. Пазете суха
на думите барутницата."

Не могат кухи общи фрази
да възвеличаят Майка Рус,
- официалната ни тема –
как тя с оръжие в ръка се вдигнала
подир баташкото клане,
тогава пеленачетата сучели
кръв от майчината гръд
подобно птичета от Пеликан свещен
без мляко, без надежда за спасение.

Викът на тези духове свещени
издига се в сърцето на света

в миг мрачен, отеква в живопис,
във акварел и слово вдъхновени:
това е нашият завет, с който плащаме
за храброст, обич и трагедия.
Историята сама напомня и тананика ни
в Батак приспивната си песен.

                    Превел: Красин Химирски

Plein Air

On the road, town by town,
the mascot troubadour
studies his colleagues
as they day dream in
paint and water color
their private reveries
each vision unique as
each spirit after wine,
rakia, or simple water.

"Language," the master
told us once, "is like
water color. It blots easily.
You've go to know what
you're after and get it on
quickly. Everything gets
watered sooner or later
with tears," he said, "your
own or otherpeople's.
The contrasts want to run
together, and must not be
allowed to. They're what
you see with. Keep your
word hoard dry."

No elevated generics then
to sing the praise of Mother
Russia, our official subject,
how she took up arms after
Batak's massacre, and babies
drank blood like chicks from
the sacred Pelican when there
was no milk, no hope of salvation.

The cry from these sweet ghosts
wound its way in the heart of the
world at that dark moment, and we
hear its echo still, if blessed, in paint
and water and words: the attention
we pay to tragedy, courage and love
as sung to us by history - taking note
in Batak, of the human lullaby.

Coffee Poem

This morning, distracted,
I load the coffee filter
with oatmeal. Funny.

But I think of mother
staring out at the snow
covering the parking lot
of the nursing home,
furious at the little Hitler
who stormed into her room and
confiscated her Beno, her
Tylenol, her Milk of Magnesia.

"It's no laughing matter, honey,
old age just isn't fair. These days,
I can't even remember what I had
for breakfast, and they're so mean
to me here   " Comes down in the
blood, as she would say.

So, what is the name of that guy on
the burro, Juan Valdeze, on his way to
market with the best Columbian?
He's smiling at me. Knows I need a
cup of java to load the coffee machine.

Twenty One Polo Horses Dead from Mysterious Illness

"Once powerful, beautiful athletes,
the polo ponies lay strangely motionless."

The Palm Beach Post, 4/21/09

"Man should consider himself fortunate
to have been a contemporary of the rose."

Juan Ramón Jiménez

The horses are lying in green fields,
dreaming of their mothers. They are
kicking in the warm bellies of their
mothers who stand on the icy hillside,
waiting for spring. They are lying
in the green fields, ashamed
because they can not rise and
take the bit between their teeth.

The velvet pond between their
nostrils is riffled like water before
a storm with their short breaths.
The polished agate of their eyes
cloud over like a winter moon.

They feel the burn that comes with
a day of play on the green fields, but
they can not stand for the groom who
stands over them weeping. The horses
look at each other, lying in the green grass,
one by one, aflame, as they finish their race.

Sweet Daisy and poems from
THE REVENANT

The Revenant

Daisy stretches herself out like
a mermaid on the kitchen floor.
She throws her head back and wails
for no apparent reason. It could be comic:
Her luxurious cocker ears fall in a chocolate
cascade like the Sun King's wig or a Dutch
Burgomaster. Why so inconsolable, Daisy?

The cookie jar is out of view,
There is no toy you can not reach,
no siren sounds that I can hear. I have
not packed my bags to leave you.

"They look at something we
can't look at yet," you said once
of the ghosts of the house,
"averting their sad glance when
we're clumsy with one another."

Are you playing with us now dear
ghost, tossing an unseen ball to
Daisy, trying to cheer us up a bit?
Does she see you through her
clouded cataracts, the way you
come to me at the edge of sleep?

Do not tease us please, my dear;
Come in full, if apparition. You've
left us lonely beyond measure,
turned Daisy to a banshee, and my
poor brain again, a tree of frantic birds.

Anniversary, for William

Daisy stands at the foot of the
stairwell, howling. She can not see,
despite the night light I left for her.
She knows the spiral staircase is
full of danger like someone caught
in a burning building, afraid to go
down. But her dilemma now lies in
ascent. She knows she can fall
going up, each day a little more
difficult, with the fading of the light.

So, she cries. Big, deep sobs,
because she is going blind and
stumbles for no reason. Whatever
made us believe the foolish notion
that animals don't register pain, are not
saddened by the fading of the light.

(She's spoiled, I know it and, well,
we're to blame: We'd sit on the deck,
acorns raining like little asteroids,
or shooting stars, as puppy Daisy,
unafraid, tested the edge of the deck,
or stood before the citronella bucket,
black eyes shining, curious, in the
candle light. She had her way
when she was young, like me.)

So, I flood the upper living room with light
and invite her up to join me. Step by step,
oh, so carefully she rises, where love and
security await her. Just like me, step by step,
making my way to you, year two now,
in the dark.

May 30, 2009
Skunk Hour

It strikes at midnight usually
but can come as early as five,
sitting under the two oaks,
me and you, for cocktails
where your ashes lie.

Then off shoots Daisy
mistaking the kitten, who
waves her proud flag amid the
fallen Rhododendron blossoms
for the usual cat she likes
to corner, just for the fun of it.

Then off shoots Richard
visions of tomato juice baths
and days of pungent towels
stinking up the house like death.

But Daisy's a good girl, catches
my meaning and lets the skunk
meander under the deck to safety.
Little epiphany, little grace note
to brighten the end of our day.

Night Light for Daisy

Like Hotel 6,
I leave the light on for her
so she doesn't stumble
into the dark stairwell,
and/or, I suppose, I too.

She lies like a small blanket
of chocolate curls, snoring,
a bit immodestly, but with
the forgiveness of sleep.

She lies dreaming like a
blessing, as I run my hand
through those soft curls-
the way you used to do -
to touch you on
the other side.

Sensory Perception

I said shush girl
Shut your lips
Do the Helen Keller
and talk with your hips

From "Don't Trust Me" by 3OH!3

Daisy and I don't need to talk
we don't need ESP, we have SP.
I place my finger into the center
of the five pad star of her paw,
and scratch there. I stroke her soft
head and she blinks a thank you as
she sits immobile beside me like
one of those ceramic dogs old Dave
always said were the best: no feeding,
no clean up, just perfect immobile attention.

She joins my vigil, in the secret garden,
become sacred to us now with the burial
of your ashes, her nose turned up to the river
smelling out what she can not exactly see,
feeling your presence as I do when the sun falls
on my shoulders and I know you have placed
you warm hand there to protect me against
the chill of spring till summer come.
Till summer at long last come.

6/17/09

Daisy Auf Naxos

She likes to drive, likes to sit on my lap
and co-pilot, flirt with the boys when the top
is down and we decelerate for a red light.

She likes the wind in her hair,
long ears flying in the breeze like
a l'Oréal commercial - she's worth it.

She doesn't mind waiting, hour after hour
in her little cave under the steering wheel:
She knows I have to come back sometime.

So, she raises hell when I take the keys
drop a cookie for her on the couch and
tell her to guard the house.

When I get home, she's lying there
where I left her. She won't speak to me.
Two cookies lie there, one imported
from her secret stash under the vanity
just to let me know she can't be bought.

True Adventure

One day, as Daisy squats out front
having a private pee, the two
Rhodesian Ridgeback brothers,
Achilles and Hector - designer dogs
the yuppie neighbors have imported
for their summer home, wander into
my driveway looking for lions or
wildebeest, swinging their massive
heads like metronomes in slow unison.

"Ms. Daisy, I say to myself, you are
about to meet your maker - it's either
you or me honey - these boys will
have us both for lunch if I try to
break up a dog fight." Daisy sees them
dimly in the distance, thinking perhaps
they are a couple of cheeky deer
trespassing again in search of fallen
apples or planning to raid the garden.

She plants her four feet firmly and
yaps like hell to get out of her yard:
Ms. Daisy is no shrinking margarita.

"Man, this is one crazy bitch,"
Achliles says to Hector, tails like
jack hammers between their legs and
they lumber off in search of easier prey.

At the Vet

As long as I don't talk too much
Daisy lets me come into the exam
room with her. It's time to check
her skin and some female problems
with her friend Dr. Crockett.

"Hello Daisy. How are you darling?"
And they nuzzle each other like
Charo kissing Dave Letterman.

Dr. Crocket wears pancake make up,
pink lipstick and Gladiator Sandals by
Marciano Trevina. She's careful not to
snarl the pale blue sapphires, little
chandeliers which match her eyes,
in Daisy's own luxurious ears.

"Have you been to Mardi Gras, dear,"
she asks, admiring Daisy's purple beads
and collar which turn her chocolate coat
into an art deco liver color as she gambols
in the summer green at the hour of absinth.

"How's he been treating you dear. Here
try this new shampoo. I had a rabbit in for
lice this afternoon. He swears by it."

So, out we go to the pink girl at the counter,
lovely as a Renoir model, who hands me the
slip to sign. It might as well have been
botox - my credit card melts as I run it
through the slot. But Daisy is her old self
again, sticks her nose into the nose of some
old wolf who has entered the waiting room.

After a certain age, a girl has to
pay a little more attention to herself.

DAISY CHAIN

How Do I Love Thee....

She loves me,
she loves me not,
she loves me,
she loves me not -

Hell no. She loves me.

Bedtime

The field is covered in stars,
early fireflies come alive
after the rain. A fox watches
the midnight train pull itself
up the river by beacon light:
no moon, summer has not yet
smiled upon night, it is too dark
for you Daisy. Come, sleep by
the fire and let me sing a lullaby.

July 4th

Me and Daisy are getting clean.
I sit on the shower bench you sat on
as I ran the shower head over your
sweet head, blue eyes blinking,
the soapy smile. Now Daisy
bows her head patiently under
the warm stream. I turn it on myself
too, to loosen a spine that's grown
arthritic from lifting you all those years.

The guests are coming and Daisy
keeps a close eye on me, drying out
on her blanket, as I fold the laundry.
It took me years to realize why
balling the socks inside out annoyed
you so, how hard it was
to turn them right and pull them
on your fragile feet. "It's good
therapy for you," I said half joking,
the way my father might say,
"I don't care how you feel, you're
going to school today, and that's it."

The tables turned over the years.
I was severe if I caught you
peeing in to a cup at the sink
or made us late by dawdling.
Still, "I love you Ricardo,"
no matter what, came your soft reply.

So, today Daisy will stand like a
Marine Sergeant guarding the grill.
I'll put on my summer apron:
"Kiss the Chef," and sling dogs and
burgers all day under the fancy flag
the Navy gave me at your funeral.

What did they think, those cute sailors,
I wonder, thanking this old gay guy,
tears streaming down his face,
for your service to your country,
handing me this terrible freedom.

Camouflage

Daisy wears the dark
like the helmet of Perseus
when snake-headed Richard
comes prowling at bath time.

Chocolate, chameleon,
she melts into a corner or
dusts up the floor under the bed,
still as a stone in a rock garden,
a trout holding firm against
the invisible stream.

The tiny song of her dog tags
breaks the spell when she hears
me coming to scoop her up and
I know she's there the way,
from time to time, when you first
died, I'd hear you call my name and
the three of us could at last return to
sleep and the refuge of night.

Daisy Reads Bambi the Riot Act

So, what do you think you're doing
standing in the road in the middle of
the day, Bambi, you think you have
nine lives like one of Rita's cats?

Daisy yaps away, chewing out the little
baby like a traffic matron at bus time.
The fawn sighs, like Monique's bored
five year old pouting over her oatmeal:
"Je veut vivre, moi!" "Ah youth,
wasted on the young."
Daisy shakes her ears.

"Go chase some butterflies, or go down
to the river and play with the swans. And
stay away from the prison guard's field.
He shot your auntie dead last fall. You don't
want to turn into sausage, now do you?"

Daisy lumbers home for some cheese
and crackers. It's almost cocktail time,
and Daddy needs a little talking to.

The Summer of Rainbow

"No rain, no rainbows"

Every day, each more
spectacular than the last -
a gold dome rising on the
horizon, capped in prism
under a black infinity,
good and evil writ large.

Rainbow on rainbow
the double arc of dolphins
spanning the river
improbable as luck.

Band on band, color
of clover and rose
gold and cerulean blue,
the full spectrum of hope.

All summer we stood silent
like small birds hiding among
the leaves, waiting for the sun
when over head
lightening ripped apart the sky.

Getting Attuned by My Reike Master

    For Tania

The web cam eye stares back and blank,
uninstalled like the Cyclops after Ulysses.
I realize I've inadvertently placed two
blue jay feathers under the bold genitals
of Icarus who sleeps in wood among the
sculpted denizens of the library. I'm burning
and exhausted. I've only to open my eyes
and heart and wings, and I'll be fine.

Daisy spreads out like a worn out rug
puffing away at the end of the day.
A dead moth dances at the chocolate
raspberry of her nose. I must think of
such fragile life too now, it seems.

You've opened a world of angels and
guides, and other lives, who knows?
The signposts will come flooding now
like fox who stood one winter day
surveying his landscape and reappeared
the exact hour a year later when I said
the word fox. Paying attention as You did
and insisted on. Into the vortex, into
the wormhole. Why not? Powered by love
and escape from ego. The Adventure Begins.

8/25/09

All She Has

"It was definitely time to put him down. He and I
stared into each others' eyes as he died. He loved us.
We loved him. Simple and simply enough.
That's what his eyes said."

> Letter from Tucker on Cowboy's death

Daisy kisses everyone who comes to the door
Twists again like she did last summer, takes a
little excited pee, and demands a cookie
as though I haven't fed her in a month.

"She follows me everywhere and cries and cries if
I try to leave the house without her," I complain to
mother who insists I bring Daisy to the nursing
home whenever I visit. "You're all she has, honey,"
mother explains, watering the violets I brought at
Easter, now a little death valley on her windowsill.

"Oh, she's blind" friends will say when they notice
the cloudy stone become Daisy's right eye, hidden
by a crown of fur the groomer leaves as camouflage.
They're sympathetic but find it just a bit distasteful?

I look into her eye as though it were a crystal ball,
and the other as well, fixed on me with laser love:
my present and future in the sibylline face of a little
chocolate cocker spaniel. "You're all she has,"
Daisy tells me when it comes time to say goodbye
and, yes, "We must love one another and die."

Busted at Misquamicut State Park

I

Late in the day, the gatekeeper
waves me in, no charge, till
Daisy makes a false move and
smiles at him, sitting in the
shotgun seat, panting.

"Sorry guys, no dogs allowed.
You'll get arrested."

"Oh man, I'm so hot." I plead.
"Won't you let us take a dip?
We'll leave right away, promise."

"Go to the very end," he says. "I
haven't seen you. Good luck"

II

So, Daisy and I ghost our way up
the path to the ocean like
walking into a furnace or passing
through the gates of hell.
The air is brown with salt spray
and the heat of the day. Thousands
lie flattened like air crash victims
as far as the horizon and disappear,
ocean roar, the only sound.

III

We used to roll you out in a
dune buggy, yellow wheels
as big as umbrellas, like a
lunar modular vehicle, straw
hat for a space helmet.

The water was calm, blue, cool.
We drank white wine and left your
quad cane at the water's edge,
pretended gravity didn't exist,
floating in the cold skin of the globe
like sea mammals disporting
themselves in their blue pleasure.
Angels, just hovering, just hovering.

Daisy looks at me and contemplates
the furious waves crashing on the shore.
She agrees: Death it seems has
prevailed against us once again.

"Let's go home Daisy," I tell her.
"We'll try again another day."

8/23/09

Cocktails

Little "no-see-em's" like tiny devils
begin to fill the night and sting us
out of nowhere like guilt or memory.

Daisy works the crowd for tidbits from
the little feast the guest have brought:
prosciutto and melon, moose pate, salmon,
and cheese, and eggplant, floating on
cucumber barges. She wends her way
through the labyrinth of candles we've
set out on the deck against the dark.

"This is more like it," Daisy says.
"Where did you find these guys?"

I drone on like a Mourning Dove -
obsessive: What I did wrong, how
I could have saved you. The roses
the guests have brought listen with
love, carefully, as do the guests. Their
beauty comforts. They would console:
Absolution and red redemption.

The air begins to clear with the
luxury of friendship and exorcism.

8/25/09

Day Trader

"...the dichotomy of the spiritual path and our true nature. I took my rose-colored glasses off today. And I put them back on."

Email from my Reiki Master

Every night, my new friend Juan
throws his net into the dark like
a lone fisherman. He freezes like a
small star which has fallen from the sky
into the center of his platinum web
when I flash him with my Canon-
he hangs in there, intrepid.

When the sun rises, he packs it up for
the day and goes to bed somewhere
like a hard-working factory stiff,
tending the line, bumper after bumper
till it's time to refill the lunch pail
and dream of the chassies floating
toward him, incessantas
waves from the ocean. He retires
just as I am waking to begin the
day shift, trading places with him,
the day trader, sitting at his computer,
hour after hour, waiting for the time
to strike as the green line moves up,
the red line drops, tracing the DJIA,
hoping not to get tossed into the weeds,
hoping for a reasonable middle morsel,
just a modest bite before the closing bell.

I've tried to put off my aversion to
Juan throughout the summer, but
come to see him as a brother in the
art, despite his pincers and beady eyes,
my own eyes grown a bit buggy myself.

A little too greedy, a little too grounded,
I tell the master. Too taken with sex and
ego and guarding my turf by night and day:
I'm comfortable with not being a good guy.

She's challenged by this confession,
admits she likes to fuck around herself,
promises to get back to me, reminds me
of the Buddhist monk who loves
all creatures, even the scorpion who
stings him because it is his nature, and
the monk who takes it every time,
because it is his nature to love.

She puts on her rose-colored
Benjamin Franklins, and I try
to see an answer through her
eyes without any luck. Bid high,
bid low, who knows. Tomorrow
is another dia, as Juan would say.

8/28/09

Juan

(apologies to e.e. cummings
and William Blake)

I know a little Mexican
who weaves his web in platinum
Because if he spins silken ones
The wind is sure to flatten em.

Spider, spider in the night
When the day's no longer bright
Your relentless hand and eye
Weave a scary symmetry.

Dancing Lesson

For Uncle Mowrey, Liam and Sharon

When it gets too tough, Too many
bills, too many hangovers, too many
unfinished projects and never enough
time, I think of my dead godfather,
the orphan boy grandfather adopted
who raised four kids by driving truck
and criss crossed America till his legs
grew thick as tree trunks; how his wife
despaired, sure he was seeing other women
until he finally confessed he'd been taking
dancing lessons to surprise her on her birthday.
I think of them doing the cha cha
in the smoke-filled hills of western
Pennsylvania, and I turn on the music.

8/14/09

Multiple Choice Lyric

(A. greetings, B. love note, C. poison pen, D. all the above, E. none of the above, F. a little of each)

Dear (friend, beloved, asshole)

Is there any sign yet that you are (thinking of me, still in love, full of regrets) and how easily you blew (in, me, up)? Is there any chance you are thinking of (confirming, repeating, apologizing for) this behavior and returning to your previous (communications, zeal, friendship)? If so, I am at (your disposal, feet, side.) If not, I am at (the bar, my wit's end, your lawyer's.) Have a good (day, evening, life.)

For Betsy

Rainy day, wet grass, wet Daisy.
She wants me to light the fireplace.
Better you should join me in the
library Daisy. Save a little energy.
Better to rest your fat little belly
and bones here with me. You can
dream just as easily here with me and
let the spirit of the earth have her cry.

You never met Nessy, I think, Daisy-
John's little Scottie, or Betsy, his wife.
They came to these fields in happier
days, before the flames ravaged his life
and the great towers came crashing
down. Long before William slipped
away from us one spring eventide.

Oh, we walked in the sunshine, Daisy
and the fields were a great green
ballroom floor for the trees' slow waltz.

They stir us still, John and William
support us from within, even as we
add circles of life to the core
from which we grow. Still, maybe you
are right. Okay, I'll make a fire and send
some sweet-smelling smoke into the
grey clouds above us. Let's send them
our love, Daisy. Here, let me touch you.

9/11/09

Suite Insomnia

I

    Mr. Red Plays Dutch Uncle

Mr. Red keeps an eye on me.
I don't see him, but he sees me.
Marko. Polo. Oh, I'll catch him
on occasion, high red-tailing
across the road as my headlights
slice up the curves of night. And
on occasion, there he'll be, fox
perfect, formal as a bishop, a
della Rrobbia in red, white, red,
fixing me with his black eyes.

"I'll look after you," they say,
"But be a little careful. You and
Ms. Daisy aren't the only ones
trying to make their way
through the night."

II

    Ms. Daisy's Retort

"Humpf," says Daisy. "I don't
need no uppity fox telling me how
to live my life. Go dig a hole Red,
I'm on my way to West Palm Beach
for the winter.

III

    Now Come Jay and Mockingbird
    The Sycophants of the Dawn

"Fox is right! Fox is right!
The sun is up, the river's on fire.
Brother Fox is always right."

9/18/09

Letter from Tucker on Cowboy's death

Daisy kisses everyone who comes to the door
Twists again like she did last summer, takes a
little excited pee, and demands a cookie
as though I haven't fed her in a month.

"She follows me everywhere and cries and cries if
I try to leave the house without her," I complain to
mother who insists I bring Daisy to the nursing
home whenever I visit. "You're all she has, honey,"
mother explains, watering the violets I brought at
Easter, become a little death valley on her windowsill.

"Oh, she's blind" friends will say when they notice
the cloudy stone become Daisy's right eye, hidden
by a crown of fur the groomer leaves as camouflage.
They're sympathetic but find it just a bit distasteful?

I look into her eye as though it were a crystal ball,
and the other as well, fixed on me with laser love:
my present and future in the sibylline face of a little
chocolate cocker spaniel. "You're all she has,"
Daisy tells me when it comes time to say goodbye
and, yes, "We must love one another and die."

"Honey, when is mosquitos over?"
     Mother, on a visit

In the summer, it was her pleasure to sit
and watch the traffic move on Market Street,
leave the stale air of the nursing home, drive
her little electric scooter our front, her private porch
and watch the world go by. No crazies screaming at
lunch about Obama, or their dead wife, or how their
socks had changed color in the night. No one
bent over like a cork screw, no Nazi's administering
pills or raiding her secret stash of eclairs.

But then the mosquitos came. Dropping red pennies
along her calves and ankles. Skin paper thin now - oh
how the body changes. If they only knew, only knew
the monstrosity of this fatigue, this great shadow that comes
at his will, like the little chirping of the old men who sit
out front of their rooms all day, flirting with the nurses,
flirting with the memory of some woman who
meant something to them when they were men.

Summer hasn't been kind, driving her back indoors.
This last private haven lost to her, despite the Cutters and
fancy bug sprays I've brought her. Everything is onslaught
at some point in life. I feel it now myself. My own bones
going punk, my eyes the eyes of someone I do not know.
Daisy's muted too, with her warts, and her cataracts, and
her troubled breathing. We hole up in mother's little fortress,
the three of us. Watch a movie, a game show.
We talk about the family, envision the future.

"Honey, when is mosquitos over," she asks me.

"I really don't know momma. Sometime soon,

I guess. It's fall soon. The air will clear. There will

be a frost. We'll carve a jack o lantern and light up

the dark."

Leftovers

Cookbook poets (15 out of 28 will read!) count' em! reading their poems with poet/chef Sabine reading Italian translations. She is flying in from Montespertoli (near Florence) just forthis!
        Grace Cavalieri email promoting
        THE POET'S COOKBOOK
        (ISBN 978-1-59954-011-5)

Me and Daisy missed the boat again. No poems
for the fancy Italian cookbook. No Oysters a la Daisy,
no pasta al Dante, no Godfather Delights, no
Minestrone Mussolini, no Pizza Padrone, no
Calamari Consigliere. We kept our mouth shut,
just couldn't come up with anything special.
How fancy can you get when all you have in
the larder is gin, hamburger, and oatmeal.

So, it's leftovers again for me and Daisy which
is okay by Daisy. Even if the burger's a little
green around the edges, she licks her chops and
wags her little butt in front of the open
refrigerator door. Beep, beep, beep. Shut the door.
No amount of staring will turn up anything interesting.

We read the press release like President Obama,
head in hands, as he wings back from Copenhagen.
Should he have pitched Chicago for the Olympics?
Damned if you do, damned if you don't.
"Probably would have busted Chicago's budget anyway,
honey. Here Michelle, have a little melon ball and
prosciuto, highly recommended in the Poet's Cookbook."

Still, he gave it a try. More than I can say
for me and Daisy. But the only Italian I know
is ciao bello, and ma fangou. Leftovers again.
Sabine will zip back to Tuscany with her
Salvatore and her Claudio, and Daisy and
I will sit in front of the News Hour
speechless, drinking our sour Grappa.

Little Needle from the Peanut Gallery

In my mind's eye,
Rita lumbers up
through the fieldand
comes into my kitchen,
nose sniffing the high air.

"So, Richard. What ya got
cooking? Smells like
skunk pudding!"

And sure, the chicken I had
on medium all afternoon for
soup, has turned into a black
slime an inch deep at the
bottom of the ruined pot.

"Oh Reet, a busy day. My
eyeballs turned to jelly
in front of the blue screen.
Forgot all about the soup."

Well, here I am, a fabulous aura
of stench, burning my eyes out
for my busy day's inattention.

"And Daisy and I stay outside,"
William laughs on the breeze.

Undercounted,

Unemployed

For Indonesia

That's me. But imagine the thousands
trapped under rubble, waiting to be
rescued, who will not be rescued, who
must find some way to give up hope
and life. Those thousands agonies.
Oh my God, what have you done

10/02/09

Little Panegyric for Gracie,
    Enabler of my Daisy Fix

You are Gator Aide to my soul.
Sky Blue Water for my parched brain,
a Niagara Falls replenishing my
dry heart, all seven (or are there ten)
of the finger lakes massaging my ego,
a vast ocean on which the little bark of
my poetry can dream. Fountainhead of
friendship who surely must one day
win the Nobel Prize for Criticism.
You are Grace Cavalieri, the Italian
Joan of Arc, whose voices do not lie, at
whose touch the grass grows green and
little babies fall into sweet repose.
Mother of the lullaby, architect of the
surreal, may you live for ever and ever.
To which Daisy says, amen.

10/03/09

Q and A

Q

Debriefing: To Juan Your
(twelve) eyes only From
the pre-Aurora shift

"I beg your pardon Mr. Moth,
Who do you think you are?
Ms. Bat? Hitting me in the
forehead like that with such
spunk. Pity, Juan seems to
have gone south for the winter.
He'd teach you a thing or two."

Where is my companero Juan
when I need him. Juan, come
of hiding for a few nights, okay?
Or, I'll catch one of your grand
kids next spring and you know...
So, I'm counting on you buddy.

A

You threaten my family, you
make a big mistake, hombre.
My boys'll come from LA,
Chicago, the Bronx. Your house
gonna look like a big tent man,
we gonna roll you up into one
fat fucking enchilada. And that
little dog of yours is gonna be
mince meat, man. Don't you be
talking about my grand kids, man.

Now, where's this killer moth
you been griping about

Winter Verse for his Brother

"The day is colorless like Swiss characters in a novel
And I sit at a desk in an old house left to the arts. "
William Meredith: "For Guillaume Apollinaire"

I
The little birds of winter
march across the dead lawn
like Sherman's infantry
scavenging the fields of Georgia.

They bob and rise and make
no sound. The sun hides
somewhere down the west,
the empty sky makes no gesture.

How you loved them,
as they sat silent on a wire,
or fed at the water's edge. How
you worried after them in winter.

II
Daisy snores before the fire and
dreams she is lying in your lap.
We are driving through an
orange grove, rag top rolled back
the air heavy with orange blossom.

Some miles more we will be home,
the air turn crystal along the
aquamarine shore. But now we
wander the dead fields of winter
with the little birds that led you
on in such compassion,
such joy in life.

Eventide

In Memoriam,
Stephen Schafer 2/5/10

I

I lie on the seawall under a
Georgia O'Keefe sky, a high
checkerboard of clouds
floating out to sea above
the grey and golden underbelly
drifting west to catch the sun.
Below, the still water has turned
to onyx with the fading of the light..
I am the horizon line dividing
air and water.
                Daisy sits erect,
still as a lawn ornament, pensive.
She sniffs the air and will not take
a penny for her thoughts - what,
she thinks of today's headlines,
for example, the Fatal Shark Attack.

II

Everyone loved the beautiful kite boarder,
flying high like Icarus, bouncing off the
waves and up again, unaware in his joy
that he was tempting fate and baiting
the monster below.
                The lifeguard took his
sweet head into the crux of his elbow
and sang to him as he towed the ravaged
boy to shore. "You'll be okay," he said,
lying, as I did to you on your deathbed.

"I'm going to faint," the boy said, his life
unwinding like the scarlet ribbon reeling
in the shadows that trailed after them,
dark clouds in the water below.

III

Tomorrow, a hundred surfer boys
will take a rose between their teeth
and paddle out in defiance, in memoriam,
grieving for the loss of this youth and
their own. The sea has schooled them
in their first adult lesson of how fragile
we are, how the line that ties us to life
is severed in an instant by a shark's
razor teeth.   And how shall I learn to
recreate myself after our beloved's
death, Daisy, before the line snaps
and sky and sea merge forever?

Daisy keeps her counsel, silent
as the Sphinx. "Only look, Daisy.
See how the sickle moon is rising,
and there, the evening star. What
shall we make of this mystery, this life?"

Sex Education

A classic American beauty,
a Tab Hunter sort of look.
Blond hair, blue eyes, perfect
teeth and goofy grin. Business
School, not the College.

We were sophomores,
discovering our bodies,
preening like senior peacocks,
outdoing each other with lies
about our sexual exploits.
Learning the ropes by
gossip and porn films.
"I've heard if you stick your finger
up your ass when you beat off, it
feels good," he ventured one day.
Dreamy and dumb, always late for
breakfast, hiding a tell-tale hard on.

We all thought this was hysterical,
and dubbed him Back Door Bobbie.
Real men kept a tight asshole, that
no man's land where the sun never shines:
The asshole never even crossed our minds.

How many years did I waste, marooned
on the arrogant little island of my ignorance
while every morning, Back Door Bobbie
set solitary sail on the high sea of pleasure
hand at the tiller, taking himself over the horizon,
in full command of his beautiful vessel.

Autumn on the River

"Downriver, other dogs take up the work.
They are clearing a path for the barges of cold
and silence which the creatures are expecting."
William Meredith, "Winter on the River"

My head drinks in the pillow, the phylactery is full.

The provident geese have all flown town, the lazy

swans dawdle on, oblivious. The cricket plays to

an empty house. A battalion of bees has

commandeered the humming bird feeder. School

busses careen around the countryside like

yellow dragons. Red bleeds into the maple

bright as a warning flag: Here she comes,

here she comes. Better get off the track

Autumn comes barreling down

with barges of ice sure to follow.

Time to buy some No More Tears and

shampoo my baby-thin hair.

Time for a cap and scarf, time to air

the moth balls and assess the damage.

Time to repair, transplant and harvest,

time to nurture the heart

till spring once more revives.

The Cricket Sings the Blues
Que Sera Sera
Eat, drink and be
merry, for
tomorrow we diet

We danced the night away
under the electric moon.
Music was as easy as
crossing your legs,
love, a non-stop friction.
Stars exploded anywhere we
looked across the majestic sky.
We seized every minute of the day.
We ate our fill, at will, from
the earth's resplendent bounty
and we lost ourselves in the
endless kiss of summer.

Now fall comes roaring in
in his pimpmobile
to shut down the party
and collect the rent.
It's all soggy confetti
and stale beer. The drummer's
split, the fiddle repossessed.
All we can muster is an
arthritic squeak for the bored
clean- up crew mopping the floors.
No place left to crash, the sun
bears down like a nasty hangover.
crows line up in their black robes
and caw from the tops of trees:
"get your ass out of the garden,
and get a job" to we, who only lately
were the very definition of delight.
Oh man....

Grace

Thank you Lord for the
purple in the onion
in my salad, for the charm
and black depth of the eye
peeking out behind the
bangs of my little dog as
she begs, for the taste of
garlic, the chewy pasta,
the velvet relaxation of this nice
Shiraz. Thank you that I can
cook, and enjoy and digest.
Thank you that I am learning
how to eat alone, and that my
faith in just desserts abides.

Dear Grace,
      A little too much gin, I write something like a country western song (and the music). But I can't get through it without crying when I sing it to myself. I'd like to give it to Willie Nelson. Xx R.

    Wind Over Water
Like a wind over water
The tide in the sea
Your spirit still moves me
Though you're gone from here

When the wheat field is waving
And the clouds dance above
Your love it protects me
from pain and the grave

So blow on me darling
Rekindle my fire
Let memory take us
The heart's full desire

We'll walk in the valley
The mountain's high bliss
I give you my soul dear
This eternal kiss

I'll carry you darling
forty days forty years
time hasn't the power
to dry up these tears

For like a wind over water
The tide in the sea
You spirit still moves me
Though you're gone from here

Post Coitus
at the Texas Roadhouse

When Patti's putting on her panties
and straightening up the bed, I like
to take a dip in the clothes optional
pool out back and talk to the toads.

They was gonna put them on the
dangered species list, but the little
fellas are doing just fine now.

They sit at the edge of the pool, eyes
big and black as the Texas sky, black
as Patti's eyes when I come inside her
and we clench up together.

They don't say much, just sitting there
relaxing, even when I blow a little reefer.
The motel don't use chemicals so the
lady toad eggs just float down the drain,
and into the stream - natural. We got a lot
of toads now.
                              Each of the girls
has her own cabin so its homey.
Patti's got Virgin Mary candles
all over the place, Riki Martin pictures
and a Mogdiliani reprint. She takes off
her silky bra, and sweet brown pears
fall for the picking, then come those pink
panties and I'm at the door of heaven.

After, I fall back down, and join the
chorus. The night is body temperature,
the water green and shiny on my chest

eggs floating out to the Gulf like
dandelion on the wind, my seed bursting
like shooting stars inside my sweet Patti.

The Mind

"The mind waiting for snow is the true mind."

William Meredith

It is the reptile in us
that knows the sun has died,
that soon the rocks will turn
blue and lifeless.

It is the fortune teller's ball
on the verge of turning crystal,

the fertile clouds
about to spill their seeds
like milkweed pods
opening to the breeze.

It hears a child crying somewhere
it can not quite makeout,
a door has been left ajar,
a beloved left abandoned
and accidentally forgotten.
In a moment the world will
start turning again, a lone blue jay
screams a singular warning on the air.

The sky will break, the mind will
awake from the dream which has
been tempting to nightmare which
slithers back into the rocks now
sleeping beneath the snow.

Meanwhile, Condo President goes Dada (rhymes with gaga)

I

Hi Jack,

I'm around all day tomorrow if you have some time to discuss these questions. A hassle for us all. Meanwhile, some late night thoughts and, regards:

A lien on the condo would mean sale or purchase in the condo would be precluded, I think.

Has any of the suggestions I made been implemented?

Are fire alarm systems being replaced? That is, has any installation begun on any of the apartments in question?

Has the attorney determined who owns the other two apartments we don't own, and what our legal responsibility is if we do nothing to bring the alarm code up to date on those apartments.

                            Email to the Vice President

"In brief , at 12:00 am - I'm surrounded by idiots ! Real idiots !   I need the mafia to get things done."

                            Email from the Vice President

"Bring on the bats!"

                            Email from the President

II

Vice President, Like Alexander Haig, threatens a coup and like Haig, is immediately exposed.

President withdraws to his imagination: CONDOLAND! Imagine: the politics, the sex, the drugs, the deaths, the hopes, the aspirations, the births, the creations, the whole nine yards.
©, The President.

Last night Dick Allen read five short Zen poems that end in "snow", i.e. that is the last poem. And if you understood the five poems, you have reached satori or whichever state of divine transfiguration you may have achieved in any other religious practice.

This is an unpublished Meredith poem about me. An early poem. He forgave me a lot for my youth.

a.

"He takes liberties with other men's fires and dogs."

b.

"They don't mind."

Allen has prompted me to look into the meaning of satori and wikki says it is:"all things are Buddha things" and therefore any separation between self and the universe is illusory. This is a great idea. But like Don Rickles would say, "ah, would that I have never been born, but how many of us are that lucky?" I mean it is a hard realization to come by, shall we say.

I hereby tender my resignation on grounds of temporary sanity, and wild munchie attack.

Writer's Prayer

I

Born in a grotto, laid to rest
in a grotto, between these
rocky bookends, the story
of the earthly life you
took upon yourself:
the word made flesh.

II

We read you Lord and
try to imitate your style.
Lesser authors, we take pen
to hand and sketch a rough
draft, staring out the window,
day dreaming our lives as the
bright river and seasons flow past
until we reach "the end" and
contemplate your radiant sequel.

Lullaby for David

What happens if I put bee pollen
in the chicken soup, or heart of palm
into the salad. Or another night,
heart of newt, or bone of baby,
when the boss comes for dinner
in all his metal feathers and finery.

Toil and trouble man, my roomie
tells me he hears I am dead, the
voices have him very disconcerted.

I tell him listen, buddy, I'm okay,
you're okay if you let yourself be.
Come have some chicken soup with
me honey, and rest your weary head.

None of it is fair sweetie, but I am here
holding your hand, and bidding you
good night, sleep well.

Dream Lover

(To the tune of
"I'm a fool to love you.)

I made you love me
You made me love you
and now life's water
flows through us like
water through the locks.
We drink each other
refresh in each other,
grow impassioned by the
tide swelling through us
like the dance between
earth and moon in an
eternal night of summer.

To His Muse

There you go again, as
Ronald Regan would say,
your hand on my thigh
just as I'm about to
drift back into sleep.

And somewhere deep,
once more a fire is stirring,
molten lava begins its
relentless rise. I yawn
and turn toward you.
I know it will be worth it.

Assisted Living

She has the faith of Job -
as it says, loosely translated -
in Deuteronomy, (Dr 3: 28)
Do wacha wanna me.

But she's suing those remote
control light switch people.
She's "clapped on" so hard
she's broken her wrists. She
figures she'll make enough to
visit the new great grandchild
in San Diego. May she'll go
on Oprah, and win a new car.

She feels like a hamster running
up and down the halls in her
electric scooter. How much
bingo can you take in one week?
And what kind of prizes is that?
Oreo cookies and facial tissues?

She waters the plastic flowers
and plans her day. Maybe she'll
order a pizza or run for president.
They could use a little help
down there, but they never call,
they never write as the old nun
says of the gorilla who raped her
that afternoon, at the zoo, ha ha.
"Would that I had never been born, but
how many of us are that lucky, ha ha."

She'll take a spin down to the office
and give that red-haired girl some hell.
She gets dressed for the pizza boy
who must be coming any time now,
must be coming any time soon.

The Poet William Meredith

> "This is the old, becoming grief of shepherds,
> this the way men have of letting go..."

I held his life in my hands, rare,
rare jewel lost even most to me.
How well I did, I do not know.
A mystery, mysterious still, that I
entrust to time, and other critics
and return to God with gratitude.

Poetic License

I wear it under my lapel and
only flash it when necessary.
It beats iambic, lets me see
with x-ray vision, savor the
rose, feel the night pulsing
with summer. It lets me say
all sorts of crazy forward
things and use the word love
with impunity.

Hirsutism

If you ever caught crabs
(pubis, corporis, capitis)
you would be crab nirvana.
Alopecia will never grace
your bright lexicon. Wolf
man, brother to Sasquatch,
dream lover to shop girls
around the world who long
to sleep on the longrug
of your body, electric sparks
flying from that warm friction.

Ape man, a wall of soggy
moss cascading in the shower.
A pink star lost in the heart
of the night as you bend over
for the Ivory, your secret sword
no longer secret, rising from
its furry scabbard, a lone
dark Cyprus standing tall.

Sing to my animal blood
coursing through the trees
banana man, silky friend,
flash that bright smile,
roll those white eyes
in the lovely red forest
of your face.

Orangutang me man.
Swing me up like
a sacrificial lamb.
Let's hang out,
Let's rock in the
breeze and fall
asleep under the
moon, wrapped
in arms long
enough, strong
enough to hold
each other and
our dreams.

CGD*

It used to be a vicious Doberman
coming out of nowhere as I jogged,
the daily nightmare, a Jungian field day,
as you fended off crisis after crisis.

Now death has solved the final crisis
and I am training myself how to live:
How to eat, how to speak, how to love.

But the world is too
heavy with reference.
Memory is like a pitbull
that will not unclench his jaws.

I watch the charming story of
Maruge at 84 who joins the
first graders in Kenya to learn
how to read. Teacher Jane writes
out the word on the blackboard
for the children to fill in the
blanks as I sometimes
did for you after the stroke:

h_me, ha__y, h_althy.

Why didn't I do more?
An hour a day with Jane's
patience, herdedication?
You might have finally read
the newspaper and not just
looked at the photos.

Spell g_uilt, los_, Lone_ly, s_d.

The pit bull has me by the wrist.

Years later I still can not

spell g__dbye.

* Complicated Grief Disorder.

The current experience (more than a year after a loss) of intense intrusive thoughts, pangs of severe emotion, distressing yearnings, feeling excessively alone and empty, excessively avoiding tasks reminiscent of the deceased, unusual sleep disturbances, and maladaptive levels of loss of interest in personal activities.

Miniature

To be sure it hadn't been stolen
from its winter bed beside the barn
I walked to the point as a last resort
in search of the missing kayak.

Early summer had thrown a green
caftan over her as she slept, another
black mark for the navy boy who took her
dancing and didn't bring her home.

The water was dark as onyx,
a lone swan bobbed for grass
just off shore, the horizon divided
into blue and green - irresistible.

Not as deft as in earlier days,
I slipped into her like an old lover
and we set out together in silence
the water singing to us as we cut

the swells of a passing jetski -
a girl and boy, two boys?
holding tight as they zipped up river.
Two dragonflies in media res.

Peace on careless sailors, speed daemons.
To everything there is a season. A time to
drift, to be alone, neither sad nor happy

like the swan gliding away as I return.

I lift her ashore, and an impatient
stow away jumps from the kayak
and scurries into the bushes. A sweet,
dark-eyed mouse, a little grace note
from the universe to end the simple
song of a summer afternoon.

Turning 65

"Ask not for whom the bell tolls..."

She's going bald, she's going blind,
She will not leave my side.
I've become my guide dog's guide
as her final days unwind.

I take her shopping and to the vet,
I have a permit for the p.o.
People open the door for us,
and pat me on the head:
growing bald like Daisy,
eyes gone dim like Daisy.

I contemplate the somber day
when I must put her down.
But who will be there down the road
to do that lonely job for me?

"Best get moving," Daisy chides me.
You're grey but you're no greyhound.
Love will find you if you're looking."
And once again my guide dog guides me.

Cosmic Circle

"It's raining men, hallelujah!"

The Weather Girls

Before the rooster crows on my cell phone,
before the shade goes up and the smell of
coffee speaks to my stomach and tells it
to get a move on, unaware my hand has
spent the night cupped about the ripe package
between my legs like a Reiki practitioner
channeling the universe, I grow aware
as does my stiffening shaft that at this very
moment a billion other men are waking to the
call of their manhood, thinking of release.

Boys in Beijing are dreaming of rice,
young men in Chicago are working their
pistons, old men in Juan led Pins fix their
razor eyes on the little pigeons cruising
the cafés, and submariners in a common
sea are awash in their salty fantasy.

It strikes me that at this very moment each
of a billion orgasms will sew a billion seeds

with released energy enough to turn the globe
and outdo the sun. I stand on line with a billion
shining brothers about to take the plunge.

A boy from Argentina reaches over to touch
my left breast, and I join the sweet flow.

Podiatry for Justin Bieber

Justin I am no pederast
Justin I love your feet.
I contemplate your toes
the way they say a person's
nose will mirror his other
anatomical parts. Throw me
not your room key, throw me
not your tighty whities. Justin,
throw me a sock.

Oh pretty in the moment of
pubescence, your mother may call
you a young man. You are not.
You are a delectable old boy.

I join the hoard of Bieber girls,
the scream heard round the world,
as though ravished by a young god
and they not even teen aged yet,
sensing for the first time,
and terrified to know it, how
uncontrollable this life we're given
how at the mercy we are of love.

911 119

They
Were
Their Once
Spirit
The   And
Marvel   Those
Of   Who
The   Fell
Earth

          Eter
          nal
          Rise

"That little flower growing out of rock..."

    Margot Parrot from Catherine Hull's obituary

The small, the rare, the beautiful,
this was Catherine's talent,
what she saw in plants and people,
despite her large sophistication,
her blue blood, perhaps because of it?
How all of us rose - friends, family-
from that bedrock compassion,
despite the sometimes tempest -
like weather bearing down on us now.

The admiral takes her hand: "Katrink,
my darling, shall we dance?

Busy

> For Michael and Tamara
> who give shelter in the storm

Every morning as I rise,

my mind's a field of fireflies.

I punch holes in a jelly jar lid,

add some grass, and go gamboling.

In an hour their little hotel

blinks brighter than the Vegas strip:

Cirque de Soleil, trained tigers,

naked dancing girls,

what to choose from ?

But the dog is begging for breakfast,

the bills are raising hell on my desktop,

a food fight rages in the fridge,

the dirty laundry is sprouting mushroom.

By noon all my electric playmates have

burned out and are taking a siesta, save

this little fellow flying off the page

into your hands.

Animal Trainer

"Just don't act like a deer
and you'll probably be fine."

Tiger Trainer, Eric Orkney

Oh, Eric, I would turn my white butt up
for you, man. I'd go for the salt in your
crotch, and nuzzle you anywhere I could
get my tongue in. Blink, blink, maybe
you would kiss my dark eyes, stick your
finger into my delicate ears. Eric I bend
my head to the ground, touch me as you
wish, but don't play too rough please,
unless you want to. You've got me
frozen in your headlights, man. I'm
stunned by your knees, your thighs, your
shoulders. I'd hang my head over the
fireplace for one of your smiles.
I'd wear a yoke and pull your wagon.
I'm standing here down wind, Eric
under the apple trees, waiting for you.

Daisy wakes from her Nightmare

"He didn't come back, and he didn't come back and the skunks smelled so bad and the crazy neighbor lady kept talking about, "is it time," and he just kept falling into his computer screen like a vat of wine, and the moon was on fire, and I wanted to call 911 but I forgot the number.

Boot Camp - Cassis

Ten o'clock. Ugolino gone. The Cardinal
called back for talks in Rome?
A Camargo plot afoot to crown a female
Pope? Tant mieux. I'm coherent again,
sanity restored like a Korean POW whose
psyche has been cleansed with REM sleep
once he's finally confessed and the lights
have been turned off, finally, for good.

"I was James Bond." - recapping the dream
to a chum over coffee - "Had my own helicopter.
General Petrov, my pilot. Handshake like a vise,
 We were on an important mission, but
stopped off at a circus camp first. The General
was dressed like Liberace - see-through pajamas,
silk. He did a few hand stands to impress me
then the whole camp stood in awe, speechless
as we pulled out in our big Sikorski, silent
as a snake through the tall grass. You know,
I should have been a spy."

"No Glasses," my friend counters.
"They don't take spies who wear glasses?"
"That's right. Only sunglasses."

So everyday you'll find me at Cafe Coquillage

Behind a plate of mussels and standard issue

Ray Bands, rehearsing my new career,

Poireau en Provence, sleuth extraordinaire.

"The sun shines 400 days a year here,"
the waiter winks and spills the wine,

distracted by a busty pieton causing

a traffic jam in the street. Everybody's

on the balcony, taking her in. Coiffed

and sewn into her day suit with color-

coordinated poodle and accessories, the lady is

packaged tighter than a family-sized mozzarella

at the cheese counter at Super U. I am stirred by

not shaken and raise my glass as she passes,

still waiting for D. and S.

who rumor has it have discovered

a secret French connection

to the 12th and 25th centuries.

The ferry boats come and go with their

cargos of tourists and stolen plutonium.

But no sign of D. and S. yet. P. sits at a table

next door, Cafe Mecs, Ray Banned himself,

nose behind a book, brutalizing stupidity

through the beloved forehead of his Rene Char.

Teenagers drift by, caps turned back on their heads
like ducks taking a nap along the pond's edge,
their headset radios, two-way in reality, cueing
the commandos quietly scaling the batterie
where M. stands like an admiral in Napoleon's
old digs, scanning the sea for interlopers.
He fixes his telescope on the jet ski boys
chain sawing across the water all day long like a
nasty neighbor's lawnmower on a Sunday morning.
He misses the forest of archers scaling his cliffs for
the grenades tucked in the young men's wetsuits.

I put my chum into our Aston Martin and wheel
up the hill to the villa to check out the midgets.
 Fiendishly clever the little darlings, finger paint and
crayon code hour after hour on the Chinese terrace.
Morning doves, camflouaged color of dawn
hop up on the stone table, coo their approval,
and fly away home with their secret messages.

Cap Cannaille glows like a giant pink tiki as the sun
does its nightly tangerine thing over the Mediterreanean.
S. gathers the midgets up for supper, and D.
puts off deciphering "otherness" for a Kir royale.

Taking the Auspices

I have had on this funny suit for years, it's getting

baggy, but I can still move all the parts.

"Where He's Staying Now" - William Meredith

Oldbodies, he calls them affectionately

as he towels his own in the morning

in front of the mirror, not getting any flashier.

He thinks about Titian and Renoir a lot

in this connection. Nothing is unseemly

that takes its rise in love. If only his energy lasts. -

"His Plans for Old Age" - William Meredith

Out of sorts of late, I call my local shaman
for a little dry cleaning of the soul. Lust,
sloth and envy have me by the throat.
I need a little help to drive the devils out.

She calls the four winds and shakes her
rattle over my bones, up and down
until I begin to see the pattern in color
behind my dreaming eyelids. She's good
this witch doctor. Doesn't bother springing
forward or falling back, runs on universal time,
and sees a lot. Synchronicity's her middle name.

"What's the deal with these birds," I ask her
once I've been officially "illuminated." "No matter
where I park, both sides of my car are covered
in bird crap every morning. It's like Niagra Falls."

"They like to look at themselves in the mirror,"
she says, and sure enough, as I finish my shower,
I spy them from my bathroom window flopping around
in front of the side view mirrors, like me in my bed
every morning, waking to the body's call to prayer,
"singing the body electric," as brother Walt would say.

Sibylline, she reads the birds as easily as she
reads me. I stand preening in front of the mirror
like a stupid grackle in the throws of his vanity
jealous of youth, deaf to love, drained of vitality.
It's time to wash the car, change my sheets and
follow the humming bird south. Time to refurbish
the nest and blow on the sparks the witch has sown
in my heart to light the way as dusk approaches.

11/9/2011

Poetry

"Wine is bottled poetry"

Robert Luis Stevenson

Poetry is a woman rising
on wings at dawn, the sun
making love with the vine.

Poetry is wine to the gods.

Waving to Winter in Spring

Like Gatsby mesmerized by
the green eye blinking on the
far shore, I stand pondering
what might have been,
your smile floating
across the fullmoon,
the water, the night
gone golden, golden, gone.

Ave Maria Redux

(In this hour of the war on women
and as we approach Mother's Day)

When I was a boy and prayed
"Blessed is the fruit of thy womb,"
I always thought fruit of the loom and
let my mind wander south, mea culpa.

But there she was apparently,
a stay at home mom, looking after
a child with special needs and
not sure where he got it from.

Or maybe she sold bread
to people in the street,
to help ends meet, who knows?
We still call her blessed

who as she raised him
let him grow according to
his private nature, achieve
his private destiny.

I look at my own mother
fading now, and revise the
prayer with these small
years I've added:
Hail Mary, full of grace,
the Lord is with thee.
Blessed art thou among women
and blessed is the sacred
flowering within, Jesus.

Holy Mary, Mother of God
pray for your imperfect sons
and daughters, now and at
the hour of ourrelease.

Poor Reception

"I can't hear you. You're cracking up."

    Mother on the cell phone

Mother my mind wonders,
I'm not sleeping well.
I can't pay my bills.
Mother, I've lost my job
and been denied food stamps.
Mother, I've bought a gun
and am about to end it all.
Mother, can you hear me now?

Mother I can't get it up.
My testosterone levels
have fallen off the charts
and my hair is getting thin.
Mother the IRS is after me.
I've got a nose around my neck
and am standing on a soap box.
Mother, can you hear me now?

I can't find my glasses
or my medications.
The mice are eating the rice.
The roof is leaking and a
storm is on its way. I'm
standing on a bridge looking down.
Are you there Mother,
can you hear me now?

I'd come visit, but I've lost my car keys.
I can't afford the gas and my battery is dead.
My tags have expired and the cops have
stopped me twice. I'm due in court Monday.

Otherwise, things are pretty much okay.
Next time you call though,
you'll probably get voice mail.

Ars Poetica

What if I say you are a chambered nautilus
of potential, that your soul has a thousand
tiny ears to hear my words, and this particular
image does not lodge in any of the sweet chambers
I wish my tongue to seduce, would you help me out
and create another? Shall we say aviary, my words
lighting like a rainbow of blue jays, cardinals, and
yellow birds preening themselves in front of tiny mirrors.
Say tucan, parrot, parakeet. Say cockatiel, macaw, and
simple finch. See how they come alive in living color?

Or will you agree to be the beehive, my thoughts fermenting
on a million tiny wings, working, working, working all to
pleasure you, my queen. Write me and let me know if you
have a better idea. I want to be the best I can for both our sakes.

And if, like Cyrano, I can help you find the words to show
your inner beauty and woo your particular Roxane, we will be
even. If I say, "tell her she is more beautiful than the evening star,"
and that doesn't do the trick, come up with something better.
It's a pretty game, play it. And no matter what you come up with,
she or he will love you for it. Poetry, like life, is interactive,
and it's your poem, after all.

That's What I Like about You

I like your eyes: blue,
mirroring mine, sky
on ocean. I like your
wings, or scapulae, or
whatever they call them.
And the little joke you
make out of your walk:
"I'm a banty hen, I'm
a rooster boy, I'm a banty
hen I'm a rooster boy."
Or the sneaky way your
humor can prick some
pompous Palm Beach
windbag. I like a lot of
things about you, but
maybe not least of which is -
Say it! As Elizabeth Bishop
would say, your freight train
teenage, Dick.

The Onion Knows
The Chef is Thinking Salad

The onion is ambiguous.
He knows he's not doing
anyone any good lying
on the shelf growing soft
and mushy, sprouting
a greet tail from
sheer boredom.

But he's nervous
about the sou chef
standing like an impatient
surgeon all white coat and
knives. The stoic patient,
however, he delivers himself
up into the hands of fate.

Then, zip! Off comes the
purple overcoat, the brown
undergarments. He gleams
white and silver in his
nakedness. Then chop, chop,
chop, chop, chop, chop, chop: Oh,
Lucy in the sky with diamonds!
The onion falls to pieces as if in
orgasm. Anyone in range weeps
with onion joy. Even the dog is
barking for a piece of the action.

The onion falls like a gentle rain
onto a plain of carrot, radish and
heart of palm, lost to himself
like the Buddha in a green
and fragrant brotherhood.

Gay Blues

We found each
other one shining
day despite the fact
that people called
us gay.

We stayed warm
as the world kept turning,
throughout the cold
our love was burning.

How could I know by
spring we'd grow apart,
that a woman's beauty
would steal your heart.

I hold you in my arms
But you aren't there.
Your love has disappeared
into the thinest air.

How can I prove
that I love you the most
when the man I'm holding
is nothing but a ghost.

Time collapses contemplating the anniversary
　　of William Meredith's death today

Tempus Fugit
　　I
　　As I was a boy
　　playing with toy
　　airplanes he flew
　　among the stars
　　alone in a black sky.

　　Perhaps he heard
　　the crack of radio
　　communication,
　　perhaps not, he kept
　　himself entertained, on
　　course, and finally,
　　home.

　　II

　　Now a decade older
　　than he was when
　　we first met, I see him
　　eating a sandwich,
　　master of the seamless
　　ocean, plotting his way
　　by constellation:
　　like poetry,
　　a lonely business
　　like perhaps his aphasia
　　or whatever hard human thing
　　you can imagine,

singing alone
with a sandwich
among the stars.

Notes to the Dog Sitter

She doesn't hear or see much.
She relies on habit and smell,
and her sixth sense, which is
love of me. She'd follow me
to the moon or the water's cold
depth. So, I guess, you need to
be sure she doesn't go looking
for me. And see she has her
leash to be led and guided by
when she isn't sure where,
or why the destination.

        Mostly,
she'll be okay. She'll lie and rest
and wait, "as dogs have agreed to
do" until I return. If she howls,
it may or may not be on my behalf,
she'll stop eventually. Food and
water and her medicines are all
she'll need.

        But, pay attention to her,
she's really a great teacher. A sly
old girl, and sweet. She'll train you
how to throw a ball, or fill her bowl,
or overcome grief. There's solace in
her little pink tongue, asking for a drink;
she's a good listener, and if you listen
back, she'll tell you what she thinks.

Gaffe

Shaleeta is always late: CPT*,
to be politically incorrect.
"Say hi to William," she always
says, when she says goodbye.
Has she forgotten he's been
dead all these years now?

Spacey Shaleeta, are the stars
burning out in her grey matter
(which, like lips or vulva are
actually pink apparently,
regardless of race), or does
she take it for granted that I
commune with him after death?

Does she assume he comes to me
at the edge of consciousness, or in
the delicate buds of the variegated
beech burgeoning into pink lace
each spring, the wind stirring the
crowns of two giant oaks in a noisy
dialog high along the Thames when
ice begins to thaw, and the whale road
is once again passable. Can she guess
how he echoes in my life, how like
a duckling I've been imprinted with
the model of that life and character
as sure as the DNA which has turned
my eyes green, and provided strong
trunks on which to stand. Inscrutable
Shaleeta, mopeing her way through love.

* Racist anagram for colored people time.

Second Shift

My little dog is going blind.
Now I'm her service person.
The lenses float like wayward moons,
lost in the blackberry jelly of her eyes.

Step by step she climbs the stairs
when she's certain I've gone ahead:
a gentle leash to guide her here or
there, and keep her from bumping
into the night - lest skunk or bobcat
give her grief. My sweet Casandra,
leading by heartstrings,
showing me the way.

Euthanasia
For Dr. Sicuranza

Daisy was willing, no matter what. Willing
to let me poke into the foul putrefaction hidden
beneath the velvet chocolate of her ears, the
blood trickling and matting her chest. Willing
to let me see for her, would look right up at
me when I dropped the oily medicine onto
the opaque moons of her eyes. Would let me
lift her fat body into the tub, the tumors grown
like handles by which to lift her. And willing
to let me try my hand to expel the anal glands
that had her scooting and swirling like a top.
She didn't mind if I played doctor and tied
off a polyp, hanging like a pink tear below
her eye with a thread till it fell, black, like a
dried bean or dead tick in her bath water.

She'd sit waiting at the door till I rose from bed
to let her find her way in the field. She'd beg,
it's true, anytime the fridge door opened and
it was clear someone was eating something.

And for all this, she was still the wise counselor
who spoke for me to William after his death,
was still the little baby, sitting a cross-eyed amid
the lavender flowers, or dropping the ball in
front of me till I gave up finally watching t.v.

Always willing, a kind of defense mechanism,
her charm. Willing to be my dog, no matter what.
Willing to let me take her to the gentle young
vet who called her sweetheart as he fed the
pink poison into her brain to let her sleep.

How could I go from heroic efforts to save her to killing the thing I loved most in my life in an hour? How could she teach me this terrible final lesson?
7/7/2012

Living Will

Daisy didn't have a living will.
She'd put up with any extra-
ordinary means to stay with me:
stood patiently each morning while
I hosed out the putrid ear canals,
lumbered up and down the stairs,
the tumors hanging heavy like
nap sacks on her shoulders,
meandered lost in the field,
till I came to hook her collar
and show her the way home.
When her snoring got too loud
and the rank ears wafting in the
bedroom became almost visible,
I'd put her outside and close
the door.   She wanted to sleep
beside me, had only my smell
to anchor her to life.

What I'd give to have the little
revenant stop tapping now, and
open the door for her again.

12/12/2012

The Morning After

For the children
there will be no Santa.
For the parents there
will be no god.
Forget his name,
the guy who smeared
his rotten brains
over the
kindergarten walls
afterwards.
Hose everything down,
Or burn it to the ground
In Newtown
nothing can ever
really matter
ever again.

12/17/2012

Daniel, I'm Sorry When I Visited Your School

And you looked up from the computer and said,
"look what happened!" and all I said in return was,
"Yes, isn't it terrible." Daniel, I should have sat down
with you and hugged you for dear life crying, "Yes,
Daniel, I am as lost and stunned as you are.
But don't worry, we love you Daniel and you
are safe with us now." This job, we were told
was to be left to the parents: we must be careful
of how we touch, how we love. Beware the
predator or even the appearance. The president
speaks on behalf of "all parents," he says, when
speaking of the dead children. But what about
me, who has no children or only surrogate
children, whose heart still breaks like parents
watching the beautiful blossoms fall: She was to have
been an angel in the Christmas pageant,

He was just beginning to learn the alphabet.

Remember the big ice cream cone of India
Daniel. India they say is the mother of religion.
They have a god for everything in India. Shiva is
the black mother who when she dances brings
destruction and the end of the world like a horror
movie your parents will not let you see. But sadly
Daniel, sadly my dear little brother, today we
have seen her dance. Go home Shiva, go home,
and take your wretched world with you.

In the High Country

My mother gave me a sacred
white buffalo once, carved in
valuable white stone with two
ebony eyes. I set it standing on
top of the white chest, beside
your cremains, and the bronze
Dante and portrait of the small
waters edge water bird you said
you always wished to return as.

The tiny white buffalo stands
isolate on the lacquered surface
in a field of snow, not moving,
awaiting the spring or death,
a solitary contemplation, unable
to see her friends in the blizzard.

Does it mean I love her less to
let her live her private reverie?

At the Sink

Doing the dishes on my own now,
I remember how nightly he did
the dishes after I had cooked.

He'd look at me with pride
when things were as spark and
spangle as he could make them.

"Why do you never clean the stovetop,"
was the best that I could do at times.
And he never betrayed a single note of
hurt in his loving face.

        Seeing poorly,
a little forgetful with Alzheimers or
his stroke or whatever it was finally,
he had pretty much made the kitchen clean.

Jesus, how did he endure it.

FYEO

I wish I were riding a big bird west
blasting out to a laid-back bay
to nestle with you in some little nest
the hours all filled with day-long play.

At night I'd finger the lower frets
like tuning a very fine violin.
I'd have my way without regrets
spooning with you from ten to ten.

This is a pretty fantasy
but alas it will have to wait
for a future Parisian rhapsody
and you bring back the golden gate.

Call your Mother

"The very one who rocked you in the beginning
  needed you most in the end   "

> Hallmark condolence greeting card
> sent by Rita Dawley

Got milk? Always dry between you toes.
How accurate the popular wisdom and useful.
The things our mothers taught us that first got
us going in life: Make your bed first thing
in the morning, change your under ware
every day in case you are in an accident.
Tell the truth and shame the devil,
follow your own drummer.

And the more basic lessons
we'd rather not credit as adults:
how to eat, clean ourselves, and speak.

In the end, the cliché role reversal.
The pureed meals at the nursing home,
The diaper changes. The gospel lullabies
we listened to until I took her in my arms
and rocked her into death: "Don't cry mother,
the pain medication will kick in soon.
I'm here with you, I'm here with you.
It is ok to let go."

But it's Sunday, time to call mother.
I'm out of milk, my feet are burning,
And I can not reach her long distance.

Les deux à la fois

"Quelqu'un connait la réponse à ces questions ou personne L'une de ces stupéfiantes possibilités est également vraie."

"Pas les deux" par William Meredith

" Des lapins, gros comme des maisons"
William regardant son chien se débattre dans son sommeil

Où allons-nous quand nous rêvons ?
Pourquoi le ciel est-il bleu? Si un arbre tombe
dans la forêt   Il y a des réponses à ces questions
Demandez seulement à Alice
quand elle tombe dans le terrier,
ou à Dorothy quand elle s'élève en spirale jusqu'à Oz.

Un pays dans lequel deux conceptions contraires
peuvent s'exprimer en mêmetemps
où la douleur et le plaisir puisse ne faire qu'un.
Amour et haine, yin et yang, mâle et femelle,
Les deux côtés de la même pièce que nous jetons
dans la laverie automatique de la vie
Sort la robe de l'arc en ciel, fraîche comme le ciel.
Nous mettons nos ailes et volons jusqu'en haut de l'arbre
Pour mordre un morceau de pomme
 Nous saisissons son apparition furtive
juste à temps, alors qu'il se faufile parmi les branches.
Envolés dans un souffle, puis nous atterrissons sur la douce mousse
et nous reposons sous les fougères, le ciel se remplissant de graines aussi
délicieuses qu'une pluie de printemps
et nous nous endormons avec la douce certitude que
rien n' a d'importance et tout est important

Both

"Somebody knows or nobody knows these answers.
One of those two appalling things is true too."

"Not Both" by William Meredith

"Rabbits, big as ahouse"

William watching his dog twitch in her sleep

Where do we go when we dream
Why is the sky blue? If a tree falls
in the forest   There are answers
to these questions. Just ask Alice
as she falls into the wormhole,
or Dorothy as she spirals up to Oz.

A land where two opposing views can be held at once
Where pain and pleasure may in fact be one. Hate and
love, yin and yang, male and female, opposite sides of
the same coin we drop into the Laundromat of
life. Out comes the rainbow robe, fresh as heaven.
We put on our wings and fly to the very top of the
tree for a bite of apple. We catch his sly glance
just in time as he wends his way though the branches.

Off in a flutter then, we land on the gentle moss
and take our rest beneath the ferns, the sky
filling with seeds delicious as a spring rain
and fall asleep with the sweet assurance that
Nothing and everything matter.

The Hive

"Nam myo ho renge ko"

Nichiren Buddhist chant

Life is a flower, love is the honey

Victor Hugo

From the other side of the wall the
hive is already abuzz, something like a
washing machine droning on rhythmically
at the edge of consciousness as I dream.

When comes the foreman in his black
and yellow coveralls, hammering
on the door: "you have half an hour   "
But I am not awake yet," I protest.
"Precisely. It's time to open your eyes,
and drink the roses. Nam myo ho.   "

Love passes like honey among the workers,
their wings revved up to humming bird speed
chanting with psychic contagion, the power,
of nuclear rods going critical, feeding on the
common Eucharist of their Buddhahood.

No degrees of importance, each takes his turn
guarding the secret chamber, and even I am
pushed into the forward point of the vanguard
meant to lead us to compassion and ecstacy.

The foreman gives instruction as I cling
to the hive. "You'll discover every

vein in the petal of a white orchid,
the tender stems engorged with life,
stamen and pistil will smile at you
and invite you in; only look and see and
you'll discover the sanctity of it all
including your own, if you will only fly.

    Nam myo ho renge ko
    Nam myo ho renge ko
    Nam myo ho rengeko

Post Card: Sozopol at Sunset

"A monk at the beach. Impossible!"
      Marian Aleksiev

Seagulls bob on the crimson swells
of the Black Sea, gone grey now as the
lights along the shore in the old town
come to life like so many fireflies.
The sand tractor passes back and forth
erasing the footprints of the day -
a wedding-cake knife smoothing out
waves of icing on the beach.

                The boys and girls
who played until the sun disappeared have
stripped off their wet bathing suits to
make love and nap before promenading
in the sea garden. An ice cream, a toy
puppet, some memento of their vacation
together: a picture-perfect village for the
young in love.

But the trout on my plate is full of
recrimination: "What are you doing here,
fellow? This is no monastery. If you're
fixing to solve your life, take it to the
mountains. Look at me. Do I look like
I'm complaining? Cheer up, or clear out.
And hold the lemon, please."

Arrival, or the Beginning of the End

Well, that settles it. I simply have to get up early if there is any hope of doing some work here. At about 10 a.m. the restaurant down below begins blasting out Cher, Rod Stewart, Sting and Tina Turner to attract customers. If I close all the windows it gets too hot to work. I wonder if I could find a place in the park where it is quiet. Perhaps today, I'll marshal the power of meditation and put the music out of my mind, like a yogi who can walk on fire. Now Tom Jones comes on wailing for Delilah and it is a lost cause. Tomorrow morning, despite this cold, I will try to get up, if not with the sun, well before the music begins.

I've come to Bulgaria and a small town on the Black Sea Coast to write a kind of book end to this project, a final report on what a year of White Matter Disease has produced in me and if it accounts for changes that might not normally be ascribed to just another year of ageing.
I bit the bullet and paid for my own ticket, though the Writer's Union is taking care of in-country expenses, including a week here in Sozopol, their rest house on the Black Sea. At the end of my stay there is to be writer's conference and I am billed to sing for my supper at a gallery in Bourgas. It was either Sozopol or Varna, where William and I spent so many summers and where I met Nicky, the young beauty who became part of our life for ten years until he married and got his green card. Too many memories there, too much nostalgia. Better to try another town, with new memories and ponder what my relationship will be with my second homeland in the coming years.

Does time really speed up as we age, or is it just a psychological phenomenon? What would Einstein say. If I took a rocket to Mars, I would return a younger man apparently. "It's all relative," he might say. Even gravity is a function of time according to my friend Dave. As all matter is three dimensional, time is faster at the outer edge pushing matter forward. There is no down versus up. Dave has all the equations figured out involving infinite moments in time and the speed of light, which is why the CIA is holding him hostage, he tells me.

The military implications of his discovery are too great. It all makes sense when we toke up and he draws me sketches and equations illustrating Newtonian, then Einsteinian then Daveinian physics. Crazy, lovely Dave, always on the phone with Iraq, a telescope in his living room as big as a Mini Cooper. Who knows? If the NSA can monitor the world's emails, and the CIA run its black ops with a secret budget, he may not be just delusional. "Because you're paranoid, doesn't mean they aren't after you," goes the old chestnut.

This is to be the 100th anniversary of the Writer's Union and the tenth writers conference to be held in Sofia. At another such meeting when William was alive, I got a little teary-eyed having one too many nightcaps at the bar with Nikolay Petev, the head of the Union. "What's going to happen to me when William dies, I asked him, after I had put William to bed.

"You will always have a home here in Buglaria," he told me. And so it seems. He has sent me here in his private car with Pepi, newly dubbed Pepi Pegasus and my old friend and translator, Valentin Krustev. Perhaps unwisely, I told Valentin the whole story of Buzzie, my hopes that one day I would find someone to share my life with, someone to look after me when I am an old man the way spouses do for each other. My dear Nancy who I love is pushing 90. The actuarial tables aren't encouraging, but it looks as though she will outlive me. Is it despicable of me to be so calculating? Perhaps I should be content to have had the love of my life in William and simply live in the moment, as Eckhart Tolle suggests. There are plenty of wonderful folks who are single, are living dignified, successful lives like Roberta Warren or any of the celibate nuns and priests I've met over the years. In grade school, they taught us that being single was also a vocation sent by God. Is it to be mine now?

As we traveled through the Balkan valley on our way to the sea, Valentin said he enjoyed being alone in life. But he has had his children, even grand children and is not really alone. The key I guess is learning how to be alone without being lonely, to find those inner resources to keep going, to take joy in life through compassion which is love. Pepi Pegasus couldn't understand why I wished to stop to take a picture of the endless acres of dead sunflowers along the highway. How many summers did we stop on our way to the Black Sea to fill our arms with flowers and play hide and seek like Jack among the giant beanstalks till the bees chased us from their turf and we ran back to the car covered in sap and yellow petals.

The Sunflowers

The sunflowers bow their heads to the earth,
each the ghost of a summer joy, a lover's kiss,
a child's laughter, the taste of rose and honey.
The sunflowers are weeping at summer's end
seeds falling like black rain to nourish
and renew the spirit of the earth.

When lightening rages in the valley -
neon calligraphy on the black sky,
blue augury for winter and the freeze
to follow, they stand like Chinese
warriors awaiting rebirth or are
folded into the earth from which they
rose in the eternal cycle.

In spring, they rise refreshed, a
sea of yellow pleasure for new
lovers, replicating the DNA
of our love which gives birth to
children, and joy and sunflowers.

10.7.2013 in preparation for
Krassi's 75th birthday celebration

So, old friend you have reached
your Gibbous phase, it seems.
Let us hope the last quarter
is at least 35%. An extra 10
Krassi, to show me how to
enjoy life with the pleasure
you have never failed to mount.
And a little of your human
wisdom, born of need, raised
in acceptance, and living with
living hope. K<small>EEP AT IT</small>
M<small>R.</small> H<small>IMMIRSKI.</small> WE <small>SALUTE YOU</small>!

   All your American friends

Summer Animals

Late in their life, William Carlos Williams says
he kissed his wife while she was taking a pee....

When I take a pee and the stream
flows black against the driveway
my dog walks over the stream
in her elegant grey stick legs
and knows exactly where each of
her paws, each with four pads and
a fifth for balance I suppose, is -
and walks dry-footed to the grass
under the apple trees where the deer
feed each afternoon. I am impressed, I
think man, this girl walks differently
than I, this dog keeps her own counsel
I should pay more attention to the
wonder of my little animal sister.

Advent

Along the curve of this small street in
front of the tiny houses, rainbow
lights adorn the trees: purple, gold,
green and red. A baby lamb nods over
a manger beside a red-nosed reindeer.
There is no snow, only clear air -
perhaps a star if you wish to look up.

I am living under a Christmas tree.
And in the faint distance, the sweet
slumbering sound of a train going by
calling for sleep or snow or love,
a lullaby of expectation.

Patrick's Missed the Forsythia
Patrick Dougherty (1941-2018)

The thicket surrounding his house and deck
Has gone from bud to golden flower,
A yellow wall intense enough for
A Chinese emperor or a Van Gogh painting.
But Patrick's missed it.

Forget the terrible details,
he's gone.

Young couples out for a spring spin
Will take them in with the usual joy
of the season, spotted fawns,
the lucky ones after this arctic winter
will poke their wet noses into the
blossoms to see if they taste as good
as they look. All over town, forsythia
will call out to each other like whales
singing through the oceans. Yello, yello,
yello. But Patrick won't hear them.

It was his job, as mayor of the village
To keep things beautiful, friendly.

He'll feed the forsythia in earnest now,
And every spring will sing his song -
Anonymous, but golden, along the lane
Along the river, where Patrick lives.

Friday before Easter

Why am I so moved when I see a mother

Whale swimming with the small whale

beside her through the ocean?

Now a year later

Since I whispered to her

"It's okay to let go mother,

It's okay."

      What was I thinking?

Okay to let go of your life?

Okay to let go of me?

Weren't they the same really?

Oh, this this terrible mystery

of mother and son.

Today at physical therapy

a beautiful black girl carrying

an almost nearly developed baby,

manipulates my broken elbow

and uses her belly as a kind of pillow –

inside baby Margo may kick or not –

Black Madonna smiling down at me.

Today, I spent three hours at St. Juliana's

trying to purge myself of William's death,

And mother's, thinking that the death

of Christ enfolds their deaths and my own,

future death. It okay to focus on the fact

that Christ has died today. His resurrection

Is something we think of, but on this Friday

It is only that dear Jesus expired on the cross

As we all will one day do.

Jesus looking down from the cross

At his mother, weeping below him,

What must it mean to Him?

Nike

"A graceful little goddess, the Spirit of Ecstasy, who has selected road travel as her supreme delight and alighted on the prow of a Rolls-Royce motor car to revel in the freshness of the air and the musical sound of her fluttering draperies."
  Charles Sykes

If you're looking for an early morning booty call,
Forget it. This lady is built for speed, is out of here
Like a Packard Phaeton before you even wake From
the amorous dream – off before you have her
Anywhere. One minute fixed as the Statue of Liberty,
The next, vanished, and you sitting in a cloud of dust.

Look at those bumpers, the formidable wings. She's
Firing on all cylinders and has your pistons pumping.

Goddess, slow down, idle with me here a while.
Let me park in a secluded grove for some afternoon
Delight. Let's be leisurely with each other. Take
our time. I promise not to finish prematurely.
Where are you rushing angel? Come sit on my hood,
And let me worship you a while. Cap the pressure
And heat radiating up and up and up, and let us make
An ornament of the afternoon , fix the day's pleasure
Forever in the shape of a goddess turned woman
In fleshy, slow-motion perfection.

4:30 A.M.
   for Neely

Like a newly minted mother

Who can not sleep when her Baby
Cries , I put on my shorts and tee
And lumber out with the dog
For a walk and a pee in the field.

Snif, snif, snif she will only snif
When her little cry at my door
Seemed so urgent. I stand firm
In the cool night air finally,
While she sorts out who has been
Here lately, has a bite of the last
Green shoots of summer grass.

I arch my back and there they are,
The Stars! Oh the stars man,
Piercing the black sky in shapes
Of dipper, dog and ancient heroes.

I think of my Facebook niece asking
For help with her insomnia and a
Baby who will not sleep yet through
The night. "It will change," her friends
Counsel. "This exhaustion fades as you
Walk your road." And yes, I'd add,
there are occasional stars along the way.

For Graeme Beryn's Old Computer

    2050, or So, an
      Early Intimation.

When I go to bed
I say good night
To my computer.
Strange - perhaps
2001 talk with Hal?

But how do I account for
the affection, gratitude for
hanging in there with me,
slow-movingcomputer
slow- moving mind. We
somehow get through
the day together, and
as far as I am concerned,
anything (one?) that helps you
get through the day well can be
considered a friend.

After Dinner

When we parted
Jack said:

Every breath
is a song.

Sing.

Winter Valentine

For Pat and Katria

I take out the dog, take in the stars –
there's the little dipper again -
Polaris at the top of the handle -
while she has her pee and listens
to a train passing in the night.

I like it too, this respite from
Being indoors, passing by the crystal
Heart (ruby) the lady down the hall
Has hung on her front door
in the spirit of the season.

The little girl deer who
Has come back three years
In a row, despite her deformity
Checks me out with day-glow eyes
From the center of the field,
No need to run, we are neighbors.

How can I be so content,
When the country seems so
forlorn, what accounts for
This moment of grace.

The Peacock at Bachkovo Monastery

They say I was too proud of my beauty,
And so I have been rusticated here
At the monastery. I fan myself out
Under the ancient trees to remind the
Monks, what they have sacrificed by
Turning away from the bright world
With a view toward celestial light.

Each eye of my train speaks of
Eternity to help them focus on
The future, now and ever shall be,
In the loving arms of God.

Still, I can not resist an occasional
Scream to remind them that
It will not be easy until the door
Opens and reality transforms
into the clarity of crystal.

Blow Jack, Blow

Every time I see him,
Jack tells me he's dying from
the bottom up. "Better than
dying from the top down,"
I tell him, ha ha: the organ
recital whenever two old men
hang out together. "Every breath
in life is a song," Jack tells me.
"Sing. You and I are on our way out."

I think of the train engineer tonight in
Florence, S.C. who takes his pleasure
sounding his whistle in distance,
clickety-clacking his way to Savannah,
an easy, straight shot, lolling all the
dreamers to sleep as he passes.

Sound your horn, sir. Give it
everything you've got.
Lay on that baby
like the night angel
singing his way south.

Burgeoning

When the tulip head grows
engorged for the rose,
petals will surely fly.

Mysterious centers released
till death do them part,
a little man in a boat
adrift amid a sea of tulip

Compassion

Like the sound of a train
lacing up the landscape,
grieving through the night,
a lullaby for dreamers
lost in the limbo of sleep.

Fall Moon

11-8-2017
for Jim Beall

I have for so many years
Climbed the ladder to the moon
Which flattened out on the river
And made access seem possible.

Step by golden step
Walking up to that
Completion. Tonight
Again, it beckons.

You can see your breath
Against it. It makes you
Want to straighten up your
Back and breath deep.

You know you are beyond the mid-point In
your life, and you relish what is coming.

The First Firefly of Summer

My heart sings
Bling bling, bling bling
There is light. There is hope.

Kudos for Gracie

If you asked her her age,
she might say, "Oh honey!
I'm hot! Let's not talk about age,
thus proving her response.

This chick is savvy, they might say
during the War, and it's an attribute
she wears well. Even into the present.

So, this is a kind of love poem after
living with your book and getting to
know you better, your talent.

HOW MANY LETTERS
DO YOU GET LIKE THIS!

I hope many, many Grace.

For Gracie, New Angel in Annapolis

So now our dear has risen to the heights
And bridled snowy Pegasus aloft
To sing her songs and make the world all right

With humor, love and most of all her craft
Reminding us of beauty day and night
Despite the politics of fear and graft

That overwhelms our current nasty plight
As leaders lie and shun our moral past
And make a mockery of what is right.

She'll take no crap and be the very last
One in the room to cede the bloody fight
With Fox's racist vision of the past

And yet her heart so big and full of light
Has strength enough and love to cast
Out darkness from the present dreary night

And do what poems always do the best
To heal the wounds that try to crush our spirit
And bring us closer to a world where the quest
Must be to shoulder pain and how to bear it.

Holiday Supper
    For Sonny Patrick Brennan

At Ruby Tuesday's last night, Mary,
The hostess, sat us in the family section
Which I didn't mind for the window
View I had of my new ride sitting in the
handicapped slot outfront.

There were babies galore, all on
Good behavior, dressed for the season
In stripped elf pants, baby Santa hats,
red and green jumpers, snowman pampers.

One kept his eye on me as he
Drank from a bottle, sitting on his
Father's lap, - a young dad, a sailor,
No doubt on leave. Short hair, simple
Face, strong brown arms, at peace
With his boy smiling up at him,
Thinking, I imagine, how worth it
It all was, waking early every
Morning to change a diaper or
Warm a bottle, leaving quietly
for the ship before dawn.

I watched him, like spying on
St. Joseph contemplating the
Astounding mystery, the beauty
Of the child resting in his arms.
I felt the tow of mistletoe,
Encircling the whole globe
Like stars in the silent night.

Labor Day

Sprayed

    (with apologies to Rita and Pepé Le Pew)

She's saved her sovereignty,
But lost her virginity, skunk-wise.
She is now not a dog with whom
You would wish to nuzzle.
It didn't take an arsenal, just one bad actor
Placed strategically like an A bomb under
The neighbor's deck and my puppy's gone
Radioactive. I'd best bathe her before her
exquisite sense of smell drives her crazy
the way it's doing me, before the stink
permeates permanently throughout the house
Like summer road kill. And hope she's learned
the black-and-white-stripped one is not a kitten
to mess with. Time will need to cure this wound.

No amount of burning incense or Fabreze will
cover the rancid peanut butter smell rising like
a green gas from her bedding. It's going to
take gallons of tomato juice and oatmeal
shampoo to bring my sweet, penitent baby back
to me, so we can have breakfast and play ball.

Wood Rot

My Paul Bunyan tenant has Glousterd out
The glass-green eyeballs from the plastic
Owl I have set up to keep the wood peckers
From attaching the house. He needed them
For his own craft creation, some kind of ogre
In driftwood hiding under a bridge lit up with

Christmas lights. Woody and his fellow peckers
are no longer scared of the blind bird meant to
threaten them away and guard the upper WC
wall where I am taking my morning constitutional.

Ho-ho-ho ho ho! Ho-ho-ho ho ho!
The wood pecker taps away like some
inspired jazz percussionist and no amount
of banging on the wall sends him away.
Daddy- longlegs have begun to make their
Slow march over the computer and book case.
Squirrels are beginning to put in a supply of
Acorns, and a scout bat wings in on occasion
To see if this might be a good place to roost.
Creatures are taking over now that fall has come,
And I sit here like so much wood rot, waiting
For the rains to come and later, snow.

Night Walk

We walked out into the
evening as it began to rain.
The dog turned up her nose
And wondered what these
field smells were, coming.

Grass, end of heat at the
beginning of summer and
the trees at the park's edge
waving back to us, a spirit
of gratitude floating over this
Earth at this moment.

    7/6/2019

Opioid Song

Then there is that
particular moment
When you are no longer
In pain. Nirvana moment,
No matter the solution.
Who would not?

Note to Roger

Roger gets Lisbon,
I get Stan Getz and
Ipanema. Still, a
Steaming cup of coffee
On a fall morning with
Good work in the offing
Is my idea of something
To do - I get a kick
Out of you, but envy
You and Sara too.

Triptych

I

Burgeoning in Kensington

When the tulip head grows
engorged for the rose,
petals will surely fly.
Hidden centers released
as death do them part,
a little man in a boat
adrift amid a sea of tulip

II

Vesuvius

She sleeps like Vesuvius
As I caress the rose
In the flower box
I've been planting.
A worm stirs in the heart
of the flower, the center of
every cherry in the orchard
Of my mind.
Who is giving, who
Is taking the fleshy
pleasure, this mysterious,
oneness, this eruption.

III

Tuscany

Who needs Tuscany when
poems are beginning to bloom
in the hard winter earth
of Maryland, and love?
What need a cappuccino
In a Roman trattoria
When my sweetie puts down a
French Roast Folgers on my desk?

Hard cranberry toast
Lathered with almond butter,
Or an omelette out of
Brie or ham or spinach
Before a walk with the dog
Down by the bamboo forest,
Or falling back into her arms
For a long winter's nap.

Until I win the lottery, Italy
Ain't all it's cracked up to be.
Giveme love and poetry
And a fresh morning to rise in
In my made-in-America bed.

Stopping by a Virgin Park At Dusk

The woods are lovely
Green and deep
But I shall all my
Promises keep

Until their fruit
Be ripe to reap.
Until one day
I think to sleep.

For Lyubomir Levchev

    (1935-2019)

For decades, we admired the galaxy
of his life, his achievement there
on the expanding sky of world culture.
Rare, distant, complex. How countless
were the stars and lesser bodies
drawn in by his gravity, a constellation of
poetry, politics, friendship and yes, black
matter too. Now like a comet, he spirals out
into infinity and leaves us with the sad
mystery of this diminished light.

Lullaby

Time held me gray and
fragile to his slowly beating
heart And I slept in his arms
like a dream.

Old Business, Newt Business

      For Evelyn Prettyman

When the sun warms the mud The
salamanders wakefrom their Long
winter nap and you can catch The
sleepy babies in your hand if The
spring water isn't toocold.

When I was lucky like that once I could see
the tiny pads of its feet Cling to the palm of
my hand and Meet his dark eyes – everything
so small and fragile, like wishing on a star or
finding a sacred stone before he slipped back
into the spring, chameleon like, and turned the
color of water.

      Now their tiny brotherhood,
Surrounds me: some somber, some
barking, Some laughing silently as I watch
a boy, who can't contain his joy lift a rock
and catch the beautiful creature in his very
hand To meethim eye to eye.

A Couple of Lifted Malaproprisms

Sydney

The dog doesn't digest
Meat well anymore
and Has a lot of
accidents. We'll have
to take her To the
vegetarian

Fake Gnus

You have to be a really solid

beast to take Trump's nasty

bullets.

Sunday Mass

For Mike Collins' dad
In Memoriam 7/19

I look at the purple spots
blossoming on my arms
the way this garden grew
into overgrown fields of
blood on my father's arms
at the end, his unease at
these mysterious badges
of age, and a body
beginning its
downward spiral.

The priest takes in my
companion's beauty, his
dark hair, his brown limbs
as we make our way into
the pew to prepare for
Christ's entering our soul –
Don't Ask, don't tell. God
loves the sinner not the sin

my nostalgia for my
own youth become
incarnate in the dark
eyes of this secret boy
beside me.

At his age, my prayers were
genuine, had more to do with
divine nostalgia, my wish to
make love to the moon or merge
with Christ's sacred humanity.

One by one now, friends die
and I will certainly join their
ranks sooner than later. My
prayer now, Only to accept
with compassion

the thinning hair, the dark ponds,
the turning of the globe, and that
such love will sustain me and
bring me back to the unanswered
prayer of my youth: to be
a better man, Lord.

The Indian Magi Remembers: Caspar

       Christmas, 2018

I
In an earlier youth
I experienced cosmic
Release with boys and
Men around the world.

II
And now I am in the
Sisterhood of pain
Reaching out to you
Dear, and your
fellows.

III
These all touch on where
I have been, but leave
me wanting the bright
light of an angel,
carrying the moon in her
delicate arms as she
takes her slow ladder to
the future, (rising like the
sun in the distance,) to
face the brilliant light of
day, to receive God's
kiss, His abiding love.

Walking the Dog

For Mike and Sydney

Three coyotes hover like

ghost dogs each morning

At the edge of the parking lot,

spying out the herd of deer

who come to the lick the salt –

eying in particular the one

with the kinked leg –

(From birth, a random car –

no matter, still the most

likely target for a meal

tonight.)

When I take my Australian

cattle dog Into the frigid night,

her blood is a riot of training

to guard the herd, and keep

them safe from harm.

When I walk with my herder now, as

Sirius and Mars pinpoint the winter sky,

and you manage to see through

the fog of your breathing, pairs of

day-glow retinas, some low,

some high, some on the run – a

story as endless as the Serengeti

plain - I always carry a big stick

Sandyhook Revisited

For ANNE MARIE MURPHY,
CHRISTOPHER DYLAN HOCKLEY,
and SENATOR CHRIS MURPHY

As he was learning to read

to read people, and to read

life, to know what danger is,

to know what is needed to

succeed: all the big lessons,

in came a monster, who

began slaying the playmates

the boy was beginning, at

last, to play with.

This was not a storybook monster:

real slaughter everywhere—

how could you trust anything, if you

already had trouble trusting what it

meant to be a friend, to trust his

eyes. She took him in her arms, to

give him a flickering moment of

fragile reassurance, being human,

loving each other, how we need to

play today, she lied to him--

Forthe sake of her love for him. In

his confusion, she was able to give

him this moment of hopeful

distraction before the bullets cut

through them both like a sword.

And she wrapped him up with a

mother's instinct, and they left us

like angels to the sky, to the

unknown.

ABOUT THE COVER

Title: Jehua Supai

Artist: Pablo Amaringo, Peruvain Shaman (1938-2009)

Medium: Painting - Gouache On Arches Paper

Description: Jehua Supai - Espiritus Sublimes

Here you see a sumiruna, a great maestro and man of esoteric knowledge who can transform his physical body into pure spirit. He is surrounded by a magnificent aguajal: a wet area where aguaje palms grow. An aguajal is a temple of nature, a beautiful sacred grove where the spirits like to gather.

He calls the yana puyurunas, spirit people of black clouds whose faces appear in the sky above him. They teach how to heal using the wind, the mist and the dew. They can heal illnesses arising from problems of love or separation and also legal problems.

https://pablo-amaringo.pixels.com/featured/jehua-supai-pablo-amaringo.html

Pablo Amaringo; this painting Jehua Supai is featured in the book 'The Ayahuasca Visions of Pablo Amaringo" Published by Inner Traditions. Reproduced by permission of Howard G. Charing

www.ingramcontent.com/pod-product-compliance
Lightning Source LLC
Chambersburg PA
CBHW051402070526
44584CB00023B/3259